Ratios and Other Tools for Analysis, Control and Profit

Ratios and Other Tools for Analysis, Control and Profit

David E Vance

GLOBAL
professional
publishing

Global Professional Publishing Ltd
Random Acres
Slip Mill Lane
Hawkhurst
Cranbrook
Kent TN18 5AD
Email: publishing@gppbooks.com

ISBN 978-1-906403-53-9

Printed by Good News Digital Press

For full details of Global Professional Publishing titles in
Finance, Banking and Management see our website at:
www.gppbooks.com

Contents

v

Preface

How does an investor, creditor or manager know whether a company is doing well, or about to crash and burn? From the best to the worst, there are always signs as to how a company is doing and how it is likely to do in the future.

Optimism and good wishes aside, nothing tells the tale of how a company is doing more clearly than ratios. Ratios allow a company to compare itself to its best competitors and to its own year over year performance.

Many books contain ratios. But those ratios are buried under tons of other material. This book provides a clean, simple method of evaluating company performance.

Ratios are used by outsiders to gauge a company's creditworthiness and by management to diagnose problems and to set goals. Diagnostic and goal setting ratios are particularly useful to management bent on driving a company to peak performance.

Before ratios can be applied, one must be able to read financial statements. While statements are similar across companies, the details vary enough that most have to be reformatted before meaningful ratios can be developed. Chapter one discusses how to read, interpret and reformat financial statements into a standard form.

Chapters two through five discuss ratios and performance standards for profitability, cash flow, asset management and creditworthiness. Chapters six and seven discuss staffing and executive compensation ratios. Chapter eight discusses break even analysis and profit planning. Chapter nine discusses the time value of money, computing mortgage payments and bond value. Chapter ten discusses capital budgeting, project ranking and the optimal capital budget. Chapter eleven discusses ratios investment banks and others might use to value a company and maximize shareholder wealth. Chapter twelve discusses specialized ratios and key performance indicators for a number of industries.

I have taught much of this material at Rutgers University School of Business Camden in their MBA program for more than a decade, and more important, I have used many of these ratios as an auditor, controller, chief financial officer, and in corporate restructuring.

David E. Vance
Assistant Professor,
Rutgers University
School of Business Camden

CHAPTER 1

How to Read Financial Statements

Introduction

Generally Accepted Accounting Principals (GAAP) provides guidelines for organizing, classifying, adjusting, and reporting financial information. Financial statements based on GAAP are historical in nature.

GAAP financial reporting requires four basic financial statements the (i) Income Statement, (ii) Statement of Retained Earnings, (iii) Balance Sheet and (iv) Statement of Cash Flows. The exact format of these statements, the account names used, and the level of detail vary from company to company. Since the Statement of Retained Earnings is not generally used to construct ratios, it will not be discussed further. It is only mentioned for completeness.

One criticism of GAAP accounting is that it has layers and layers of rules, exceptions, and details, many of which only make sense after years of accounting training. In this book, general principals are discussed that can be used to analyze what is going on without extensive accounting training.

Ratios only have meaning if they can be compared to something. Historical ratios provide information as to whether a company is improving or deteriorating over time. Comparative industry ratios indicate how a company is doing relative to its industry.

Benchmarking is computing ratios for a company's top competitors and using those as the basis of comparison.

Because financial statements vary in their details from company to company, it is useful to reformat and condense financial statements before beginning ratio analysis. This chapter identifies key landmarks in financial statements and suggests how to reformat financial statements so they are more uniform and easier to use.

Income statement/Statement of Earnings

GAAP financial statements require accrual accounting for all but the smallest companies. Accrual accounting measures revenue from the time it is earned, and measures expenses from the time they are incurred whether or not cash is received or paid. Accrual accounting also matches costs to the revenue they help generate. An example of the matching principal can be seen in depreciation. If a company buys a truck for $60,000 which it plans to use for five years and then sell for $10,000 it will use up $50,000 of the truck's value over the time it owns the truck. If the truck helps generate revenue in each of the five years it is owned, then $10,000 per year of the truck's value should be booked as a depreciation expense ($50,000 / 5 years).

Revenue is earned for goods when title to goods passes to a customer. Revenue is booked for services as work is completed. If a company has a $20,000 contract to write software, billable at $100 per hour, and the company works on the contract 50 hours, the company can book $5,000 of revenue. Most people think of a sale as the point a contract is signed whether or not goods or services are delivered. Under GAAP, making a sale and earning revenue are not the same. Nevertheless, in this book, we will use the term sale to mean revenue to simplify nomenclature.

An Income Statement may be labeled as an Income Statement, but it may also be called a Statement of Earnings or a Consolidated Statement of Earnings. It all means the same thing. Part of the art of unraveling what financial statements mean is to recognize that the same thing can be called by different names.

Revenue

Revenue, which will be referred to through out this book as sales despite several technical distinctions, is the first line on an income statement. Sales or revenue is an important landmark because without sales, a company has no purpose and no profits.

Cost of Goods Sold

Cost of Goods Sold (COGS) is the cost to produce goods, if the company is in manufacturing. If a company is in wholesaling or retailing COGS is the cost to purchase goods. COGS is sometimes called Cost of Products Sold (COPS) or Cost of Sales (COS). Cost of goods sold for a service company is Cost of Services (COS). All of these are functionally equivalent because they provide the customer with what the customer wants. To simplify discussion, think of all of these as COGS. Draw a distinction between COGS and period costs. The cost of the corporate office building, accountants, salespeople, advertising and all other costs not directly related to making the product or delivering service are period costs.

Sometimes COGS and period costs are listed together as expenses. The first step in reformatting an income statement is to separate COGS from all other expenses. Table 1-1 Standardized Income Statement Campbell Soup provides a condensed, simplified format for analyzing income statements. Table 1-2 Campbell Soup Income Statement 2007 is an analysis of a fairly typical income statement as published by the company.

Table 1-1 Standardized Income Statement / Campbell Soup

Dollars are in millions		
Revenue (Sales)		$7,867
COGS		$4,571
Gross Profit		$3,296
Overhead		
Selling & Marketing Expenses	$1,322	
Other Overhead	$681	
Total Overhead		$2,003
Earnings Before Interest and Taxes (EBIT)		$1,293
Interest Expense	$163	
Less Interest Income	$19	
Interest Expense (net)		$144
Earnings Before Taxes (EBT)		$1,149
Income Taxes		$326
Earnings from Continuing Operations		$823
Discontinued Operations (net of tax)		$31
Extraordinary Items (net of tax)		____
Net Income		$854

Gross Profit

Gross profit is the amount of sales dollars a company has left after it makes or buys goods or provides a service. Gross profit is a subtotal, Sales less COGS. Some financial statements provide this subtotal. But where expenses are lumped together, Gross profit will have to be computed as shown in Table 1-1 Standardized Income Statement.

Overhead

Some companies list General Selling & Administrative (GS&A) as a category and throw all costs into that category. Other companies break out Selling & Marketing Expense, Corporate Expenses, or even individual category expenses like facilities, telecommunications, and so forth. The composition of Overhead will vary from company to company as will the level of detail and the names of accounts. For purposes of ratio analysis, it's important not to get bogged down in the minutia. Think of Overhead as all the costs between Gross Profit and Earnings Before Interest and Taxes (EBIT).

Selling & Marketing Costs

Selling and marketing costs include things like commissions, advertising, promotional expenses and salespersons salaries. Seiling & Marketing costs are a subdivision of Overhead. Overhead generally doesn't rise or fall as sales rise or fall. On the other hand, Selling and Marketing costs do tend to rise and fall with sales. Identifying and separating Selling & Marketing Costs from Other Overhead provides additional insight into a company's operations. Not every company reports selling and marketing costs separately in their financial statements.

Other Overhead

Other Overhead is Overhead less Selling and Marketing Costs. While one might expect Selling and Marketing costs to rise and fall with sales, Other Overhead should decline as sales rise. Other Overhead includes things like administrative offices and accountants salaries. Since Other Overhead is not used to make or sell the product, it should be subject to strict scrutiny. Other Overhead cannot be computed for companies that do not report Selling and Marketing Costs.

Table 1-2 Campbell Soup Income Statement 2007

Campbell Soup
Consolidated Statements of Earnings
(millions, except per share amounts)

	2007	2006	2005
Net Sales	$ 7,867	$ 7,343	$ 7,072
Costs and expenses			
Cost of products sold	4,571	4,273	4,179
Marketing and selling expenses	1,322	1,227	1,153
Administrative expenses	604	583	520
Research and development expenses	112	104	93
Other expenses / (income)	(35)	5	(5)
Total costs and expenses	6,574	6,192	5,940
Earnings Before Interest and Taxes	1,293	1,151	1,132
Interest expense	163	165	184
Interest income	19	15	4
Earnings before taxes	1,149	1,001	952
Taxes on earnings	326	246	308
Earnings from continuing operations	823	755	644
Earnings from discontinued operations	31	11	63
Net Earnings	$ 854	$ 766	$ 707
Per Share — Basic			
Earnings from continuing operations	$ 2.13	$ 1.86	$ 1.57
Earnings from discontinued operations	.08	.03	.15
Net Earnings	$ 2.21	$ 1.88	$ 1.73
Weighted average shares outstanding — basic	386	407	409
Per Share — Assuming Dilution			
Earnings from continuing operations	$ 2.08	$ 1.82	$ 1.56
Earnings from discontinued operations	.08	.03	.15
Net Earnings	$ 2.16	$ 1.85	$ 1.71
Weighted average shares outstanding — assuming dilution	396	413	414

See Notes to Consolidated Financial Statements in SEC Form 10-K.

▷ Revenue and sales are the same thing. Sales for 2007 were $7,867 million

▷ Cost of Goods Sold is called Cost of Products Sold and were $4,571 million.

▷ There is no subtotal for Gross Profit in this income statement.

▷ Selling & Marketing Expenses of $1,399 million is a subdivision of Overhead.

▷ Overhead is everything between Gross Profit and Earnings before Interest and Taxes. Since there is no subtotal for Gross Profit, we must imagine one, to create the boundaries for Overhead giving $2,003 million.

▷ Other Overhead of $681 million is another subdivision of Overhead.

▷ Earnings before interest and taxes (EBIT) of $1,293 million is a measure of operating income.

▷ Interest (net) of $144 million is interest expense less interest income.

▷ Earnings before tax (EBT) of $1,149 million is taxable income and is used to compute tax rates.

▷ Taxes of $326 million are only income taxes and does not include property or payroll taxes.

▷ Earnings from continuing operations are expected to be replicated year after year and are generally the focus of future analysis.

▷ Net income is the same as Net Earnings. It is the amount of profit shareholders have earned. Net income is not necessarily paid out to shareholders as dividends. Some is retained by the company.

Earnings Before Interest and Taxes (EBIT)

Earnings Before Interest and Taxes (EBIT) is Gross Profit less Overhead. It is a measure of the productivity of a company's core business independent of its finance and tax strategy.

Interest Net

Interest Expense represents the cost of financing a company's assets. Interest income represents interest on cash deposits. If a company used its cash to pay down debts it would have less interest expense. Net Interest is interest expense less interest income.

Earnings Before Taxes (EBT)

Earnings before Taxes (EBT) is EBIT less financing costs. EBT is taxable income.

Taxes

Taxes are income taxes. Property taxes, payroll taxes, franchise and business privilege taxes are reported as part of COGS or Overhead. The reason to separate out income taxes is that they rise and fall with income and are often the largest controllable tax a company pays.

Earnings from Continuing Operations

Earnings from Continuing Operations is Earnings Before Tax (EBT) Less Taxes. It is the level of after tax earnings a company expects to sustain year after year.

Discontinued Operations

If a company has a plant, or division that is being sold or closed, the income (net of taxes) for that plant or division is broken out as a separate line item called Discontinued Operation. This line item is presented below Earnings from Continuing Operations.

Extraordinary Items

Extraordinary Items are items that are both rare and unusual. Extraordinary Items are presented (net of taxes) below Earnings from Continuing Operations and Discontinued Operations. Discontinued Operations and Extraordinary Items must be added to or subtracted from Earnings from Continuing Operations to get Net Income.

Net Income

Net Income and Net Earnings are two different names for the same thing. Where there are no Discontinued Operations or Extraordinary Items, Earnings from Continuing Operations and Net Income are the same thing. When trying to anticipate future performance, Earnings from Continuing Operations should be used for Net Income in the ratios in the following chapters.

Earnings Per Share - Basic

Earnings per Share (EPS) Basic is a ratio required at the end of an income statement. It is Net Income divided by the weighted average number of common shares outstanding. Where a company had Discontinued Operations or Extraordinary Items, Earnings per Share is computed for Earnings from Continuing Operations, Discontinued Operations, Extraordinary Items and Net Income. An illustration of various Earnings Per Share calculations are shown in Table 1-3 Earnings Per Share and Outstanding Shares.

Weighted Average Shares Outstanding

If a company issues new shares or buys back outstanding shares, the number of shares will change over the course of the year. Weighted average shares is the number of common shares outstanding, weighted by the percentage of the year they were outstanding.

Earnings per Share Fully Diluted

A company can award stock options to employees, warrants to security holders and give bond and preferred stock holders the right to convert their interests to common stock. Stock options and warrants give the holder the right to buy shares of common stock at a stated price. If all those who had the right to buy stock using options or warrants bought them, and those with convertible preferred stock and bonds converted them to common stock, there would be an immediate increase in the number of shares of common stock outstanding. The assumptions underlying such conversions are very complex and beyond the scope of this text.

This theoretical number of shares is used to compute fully diluted earnings per share for continuing operations, discontinued operations, extraordinary items, and net income.

Fully diluted EPS is an income statement ratio required by GAAP, but it is highly theoretical, and some question its value. Nevertheless, it is important to know in the event of an acquisition. If a purchasing company offers the target company's shareholders a certain price per share, they must know how many potential shares there will be.

1.3 Earnings per Share and Shares Outstanding

Campbell Soup Consolidated Statements of Earnings
(millions, except per share amounts)

	2007	2006	2005
Net Sales	$ 7,867	$ 7,343	$ 7,072
Costs and expenses			
Cost of products sold	4,571	4,273	4,179
Marketing and selling expenses	1,322	1,227	1,153
Administrative expenses	604	583	520
Research and development expenses	112	104	93
Other expenses / (income)	(35)	5	(5)
Total costs and expenses	6,574	6,192	5,940
Earnings Before Interest and Taxes	1,293	1,151	1,132
Interest expense	163	165	184
Interest income	19	15	4
Earnings before taxes	1,149	1,001	952
Taxes on earnings	326	246	308
Earnings from continuing operations	823	755	644
Earnings from discontinued operations	31	11	63
Net Earnings	$ 854	$ 766	$ 707
Per Share — Basic			
Earnings from continuing operations	$ 2.13	$ 1.86	$ 1.57
Earnings from discontinued operations	.08	.03	.15
Net Earnings	$ 2.21	1.88	$ 1.73
Weighted average shares outstanding — basic	386	407	409
Per Share — Assuming Dilution			
Earnings from continuing operations	$ 2.08	$ 1.82	$ 1.56
Earnings from discontinued operations	.08	.03	.15
Net Earnings	$ 2.16	$ 1.85	$ 1.71
Weighted average shares outstanding — assuming dilution	396	414	413

See Notes to Consolidated Financial Statements in SEC Form 10-K.

▷ Earnings per share (EPS) from continuing operations is the income a company expects to generate year after year, divided by currently outstanding shares.

▷ If a company has discontinued operations or extraordinary items, both considered one time events, the EPS for those items is separately calculated.

▷ Net earnings in this section of the Income statement is EPS from continuing operations, discontinued operations and extraordinary items.

▷ Weighted average shares outstanding takes into consideration whether a company has issued or repurchased shares during the year.

▷ EPS assuming dilution recalculates the above ratios assuming all preferred stock and bonds convertible to common have been converted and that options and warrants have been exercised.

Balance Sheet

A balance sheet lists a company's assets, liabilities and owners equity. It is a representation of the accounting equation: Assets = Liabilities + Equity. Total assets must equal total liabilities plus owner's equity. Table 1-4 Campbells Soup 2007 Balance Sheet provides a good example of a balance sheet.

Assets

Assets represent all the things a company owns. Assets include things like cash, inventory, patents, copyrights, plant, property and equipment. While companies talk about employees being their most important asset, employees cannot be owned, therefore they are not assets. The exception to this is that a company may own a contract that gives it the right to a person's service. For example, a ball club might have a contract for a player's services for a couple of years. Assets may be grouped into classes and classes are presented in order of liquidity. Those easiest to convert to cash are listed first.

Current Assets

Current assets are those expected to be converted to cash within a year or within an accounting cycle. An accounting cycle can be longer than a year if it takes more than a year to produce one unit of a company's product. Examples of current assets include: cash, accounts receivable, inventory, notes receivable within a year, and pre-paid expenses.

Cash and Cash Equivalents

Cash and cash equivalents include cash on hand in the form of currency, checking and savings account balances, short term certificates of deposit, short term Treasury bills and similar investments that can be converted into cash in a very short period of time.

Accounts Receivable

Most businesses sell to other businesses on credit. One business will call another and say, please send 50 computers. The seller will ship the computers and bill the customer. Accounts receivable represents the money that a company's customers owe it at a point in time. Unfortunately, not all customers pay up. Some go bankrupt, some go out of business, and some just never pay. Companies make an estimate for these uncollectible accounts. This estimate is called the Allowance for Doubtful Accounts.

Table 1-4 Campbell Soup Balance Sheet 2007

(Millions of dollars)	July 29, 2007	July 30, 2006
Assets		
Cash and cash equivalents	$ 71	$ 657
Accounts receivable (Note 13)	581	494
Inventories (Note 13)	775	728
Other current assets (Note 13)	151	133
Current assets of discontinued operations		100
Total current assets	1,578	2,112
Plant Assets, Net of Depreciation (Note13)	2,042	1,954
Goodwill (Note 5)	1,872	1,765
Other Intangible Assets (Note 5)	615	596
Other Assets (Note 13)	338	480
Assets of discontinued operations for sale		838
Total assets	$ 6,445	$ 7,745
Liabilities		
Current Liabilities		
Notes payable (Note 9)	$ $595	$ 1,097
Payable to suppliers and others	694	691
Accrued liabilities (Note 13)	622	820
Dividend payable	77	74
Accrued income taxes	42	121
Liabilities of discontinued operations		78
Total current liabilities	2,030	2,881
Long-term Debt (Note 9)	2,074	2,116
Other Liabilities (Note 13)	1,046	955
Liabilities of discontinued operations		25
Total liabilities	5,150	5,977
Shareowners' Equity (Note 11)		
Preferred stock; authorized 40 shares;		
none issued	—	—
Capital stock, $.0375 par value; authorized		
560M shares; issued 542M shares	20	20
Additional paid-in capital	331	352
Earnings retained in the business	7,082	6,539
Capital stock in treasury, 163M shares in		
2007 and 140M shares in 2006, at cost	(6,015)	(5,147)
Accumulated other comprehensive		
income (loss)	(123)	4
Total shareowners' equity	1,295	1,768
Total liabilities and shareowners' equity	$ 6,445	$ 7,745

Notes are an integral part of a financial statement. They provide detail about reported numbers.

The note on Accounts receivable should describe the basis for estimating the allowance for doubtful accounts.

The note on inventory explains how it was valued.

The note on Other current assets explains what they are.

Current assets are cash and all assets expected to be converted to cash within a year. Current assets is one measure of whether a company will have cash to pay its bills.

Any asset that is not a current asset is a long term asset.

Total assets are all assets entrusted to management.

Current liabilities are all the bills that will come due within a year. This is important in determining whether a company has enough cash to pay its bills.

Liabilities due in more than a year are called Non-current liabilities. Notes to current and non-current liabilities provide details as to how the numbers were calculated.

Total liabilities represent all of a company's debt.

Equity is an analysis of ownership interest.

Total Liabilities plus Shareholder's equity must equal Total Assets to balance the accounting equation.

Accounts receivable on the balance sheet is reported net of allowance for doubtful accounts.

Inventory

Inventory is all the goods a company holds for sale in the regular course of business. Flour, sugar, yeast, cookies, cakes and bread are all inventory to a baker. The flour, sugar and yeast are raw materials inventory. The cookies, cakes and bread are finished goods inventory. Raw materials that have had some labor applied to them is called work in process (WIP) inventory. WIP is inventory in an intermediate state between raw materials and finished goods. Bakers have little WIP inventory. But aircraft manufacturers probably have millions of dollars of WIP inventory at year end in the form of partially built airplanes. While flour and cookies are inventory for a baker, the ovens, mixers, and refrigerators he or she uses are not inventory because they are not held for sale in the ordinary course of business. Ovens, mixers and refrigerators are classified as plant, property and equipment.

There are several means of valuing inventory. The exact means used should be explained as a footnote to the financial statements.

Other Current Assets

The most common type of other current assets is pre-paid expenses. If a company buys and pays for an insurance policy December 31st to cover next year's operations, it has pre-paid its insurance. Pre-paid insurance is an asset. A company can pre-pay rent. That is also an asset. A company might have a note receivable, an IOU if you please, from one of its customers due within a year. That note receivable is also a current asset.

Total Current Assets

Total current assets is an important measure because it indicates the dollar value of assets that can be converted to cash within a year.

Non-current assets

Non-current assets include all assets that are not expected to be converted to cash within a year. Plant, property and equipment, patents and copyrights are examples of non-current assets.

Plant, Property and Equipment

Plant, property and equipment (PPE) includes things like land used for factories, parking lots, and office parks. Property includes things like furniture and fixtures. Equipment includes things like assembly lines, drill presses, numerically controlled milling machines and airplanes, unless the company is in the business of making airplanes, in which case airplanes might be inventory. The distinguishing characteristic of PPE is that it is used to produce the company's goods and services.

Initially, PP&E is booked at its acquisition cost. However, as it is used, its value will diminish because of wear and tear and eventually it may have to be replaced. The systematic reduction in value of PPE is called depreciation. Each year some amount of depreciation is an expense which reduces net income. The total amount of depreciation charged to each item of PPE over its life is called accumulated depreciation. When PPE is reported it is reported at acquisition cost less accumulated depreciation. Sometimes this is referred to as Plant, property and equipment (net).

Goodwill

Goodwill is only created when one company purchases another for more than the fair value of its assets. Alice Company purchases Bob Co for $10 million. The market value of Bob Co's assets are only $8 million. Alice will record the difference between the value of Bob Co's assets and what she paid as goodwill. At one level, goodwill is used to keep an acquiring company's books in balance; purchase price of $10 million equals value of assets purchased of $8 million plus goodwill of $2 million. Accountants and theorists say goodwill is a "real" asset. Banks and the average investor might say it is just a plug number. Goodwill is controversial among non-accountants. Goodwill is classified as an intangible asset.

Other Intangible Assets

Intangible assets are usually defined as things you can't see, feel or touch. Patents, copyrights, purchased trade marks, purchased trade names, and leasehold improvements are intangible assets. A more robust way of thinking of intangible assets is to think of whether there is a ready market for something. There are ready markets for real estate, inventory, used equipment and even accounts receivable. There are no ready markets for patents or copyrights because they are one of a kind, and there is no ready market for leasehold improvements or goodwill.

When a company leases commercial real estate, it usually leases space which has been stripped clean. There are no interior walls, rugs, ceilings, lights or built-in fixtures. To make space useable, the company will have to hire architects, and builders to "build out the space;" that is to install walls, carpets, ceilings, lights and so forth. The amount of money used to make leased space useable is booked as an asset called Leasehold Improvements. If a lease is for five years, one fifth of the cost of those improvements is charged as expense against income each year. The sum of all leasehold improvement expenses is called Accumulated Amortization of Leasehold improvements. The amount reflected on a balance sheet is the original cost of the leasehold improvements less accumulated amortization.

Other Assets

Other assets could mean almost anything. The best thing to do if a company has a substantial amount of other assets is to read the notes to the financial statements to see what is included in this category. If it is land held for investment, it might be quite valuable. If it is a loan due from officers it may have little value.

Total Assets

Total assets is an important landmark in a financial statement because it is the resources management has to produce income. Not all managers efficiently use assets and often companies have more assets than they need or can use which increases debt costs and lowers the amount of cash available for dividends or to grow the company.

Liabilities

Liabilities are the money a company owes to others. There are only two ways to finance assets, by borrowing money or by using owner's equity.

Current Liabilities

Current liabilities are debts that come due within a year. Current liabilities include accounts payable, accrued payroll and any loan principal which must be paid within a year. When current liabilities get too high with respect to current assets, it raises a question as to whether a company can generate enough cash to pay its bills as they become due. A bank line of credit is always a current liability because it must be repaid within a year.

Notes Payable

A note payable is an IOU. It says the company promises to pay a certain amount at a certain date with a certain amount of interest. If the date is within 12 months of the balance sheet date, it is a current liability. If the note is payable after this period, it is a long term liability.

Accounts Payable

Accounts payable are amounts owed to trade creditors. When a company calls a supplier and says, "Send 50 computers and bill me later." The company is buying on credit. Accounts payable is the total amount owned to suppliers. As bills are paid accounts payable decreases, as new supplies are ordered and received, accounts payable increases.

Accrued Liabilities

Accrued liabilities are money the company owes because it has received a benefit, but is not included in accounts payable because the supplier has not sent a bill. For example, aluminum smelters use a tremendous amount of electricity, but the electric company may not bill customers until the 15th of the month. The smelter's engineer should read the electric meter at month end to estimate the value of electricity used since the last bill. This estimate would be booked as an accrued liability.

Dividends Payable

Dividends are only paid after a resolution of the Board of Directors is passed. The resolution will state the amount of the dividend, the record date, that is the date on which ownership will be measured to determine who gets the dividend, and the payment date. As soon as the resolution is passed, the company has a legal duty to pay the dividend so it books a Dividend Payable. This liability will remain on the books until the dividend is paid.

Accrued Income Taxes

At year end, a company must estimate the amount of income tax it will have to pay when it files its income tax return. Typically companies must file a tax return and remit final tax payments on the 15th day of the third month after its year end. Between year end, when financial statements are published, and the payment date a company will have accrued income taxes. This is sometimes called Taxes payable.

Liabilities of Discontinued Operations

Liabilities of discontinued operations are obligations of the company until paid. A company cannot ignore these debts just because the operation that generated them has ended.

Non-Current Liabilities

Any liability that is not current is a non-current liability. The big distinction between current and non-current liabilities is that non-current liabilities come due at least a year in the future. That gives the company some time to accumulate cash to pay them down.

Long Term Debt

Long term debt is a broad category which includes leases, bank term loans, mortgages, and bonds due more than a year in the future. A footnote to the Balance Sheet should describe the composition of long term debt.

Other Liabilities

Other liabilities is another broad category of money owed by the company. The best approach to understanding Other Liabilities for any particular company is to read the footnote for this balance sheet item.

Total Liabilities

Total liabilities is a measure of overall company debt. Many companies fail because they let debt get out of control, so total liabilities is an important landmark on a balance sheet.

Shareholders Equity

Shareholders equity, often referred to as just equity, is an analysis of the owners' interest in a company. Table 1-5 Campbell Soup Balance Sheet 2007 Equity Section is a fairly typical representation of this portion of the balance sheet.

TABLE 1-5 CAMPBELL SOUP BALANCE SHEET 2007 EQUITY SECTION
1.5 CAMPBELL SOUP BALANCE SHEET

(Millions of dollars)

	July 29, 2007	July 30, 2006
Current Assets		
Cash and cash equivalents	$ 71	$ 657
Accounts receivable (Note 13)	581	494
Inventories (Note 13)	775	728
Other current assets (Note 13)	151	133
Current assets of discontinued operations	—	100
Total current assets	1,578	2,112
Plant Assets, Net of Depreciation (Note13)	2,042	1,954
Goodwill (Note 5)	1,872	1,765
Other Intangible Assets (Note 5)	615	596
Other Assets (Note 13)	338	480
Assets of discontinued operations for sale		838
Total assets	$ 6,445	$ 7,745
Current Liabilities		
Notes payable (Note 9)	$ 595	$ 1,097
Payable to suppliers and others	694	691
Accrued liabilities (Note 13)	622	820
Dividend payable	77	74
Accrued income taxes	42	121
Liabilities of discontinued operations	—	78
Total current liabilities	2,030	2,881
Long-term Debt (Note 9)	2,074	2,116
Other Liabilities (Note 13)	1,046	955
Liabilities of discontinued operations	—	25
Total liabilities	5,150	5,977
Shareowners' Equity (Note 11)		
Preferred stock; authorized 40 shares; none issued	—	—
Capital stock, $.0375 par value; authorized 560M shares; issued 542M shares	20	20
Additional paid-in capital	331	352
Earnings retained in the business	7,082	6,539
Capital stock in treasury, 163M shares in 2007 and 140M shares in 2006, at cost	(6,015)	(5,147)
Accumulated other comprehensive income (loss)	(123)	
Total shareowners' equity	1,295	1,768
Total liabilities and shareowners' equity	$ 6,445	$ 7,745

Shareholder's equity represents ownership interest in the company.

Preferred stock has a priority claim on assets and dividends. It is issued for start-ups or in unusual circumstances.

Par is the legal minimum value of a stock. Stock is usually sold far above its par value. If stock with a par of $1 is sold for $10, the excess over par is booked as Additional Paid in Capital.

Retained earnings is the sum of a company's net income since its inception less any dividends paid.

Treasury stock is stock that was issued and outstanding at one point, but was bought back by the company. Treasury stock reduces equity. Stock may be bought back to honor options, warrants, or conversion of bonds or preferred stock to common stock. Stock may also be bought back to increase the ownership of the remaining shareholders.

Accumulated comprehensive income or loss are non-operating adjustments for things like foreign currency translation. It is theoretical.

Total Liabilities and shareholder's equity should balance to Total Assets.

Preferred Stock

Preferred stock is an ownership interest created by contract. Preferred stock has a priority claim on assets in liquidation and a priority claim on dividends as compared to common stock. Preferred stock is frequently issued by start-up companies or where there is some unusual circumstance, like the company is in danger of bankruptcy. Preferred stock is issued with a set face amount, typically in multiples of $1,000 and it pays a stated rate of dividends. For example, a preferred share for $1,000 might have a dividend rate of 9% per year which would mean the owner is entitled to a $90 dividend each year the company has profits and the Board of Directors passes a resolution authorizing dividends. Preferred stock is often convertible to common stock.

Common Stock

Shares authorized is how many shares a company is authorized by its Articles of Incorporation filed with the state in which it is incorporated. Shares issued and outstanding is the number of shares in circulation. The balance sheet should disclose the par value of stock and the number of shares issued. Outstanding shares times par value is the amount recorded as common stock at par.

Common stock usually has a minimal par value. Par is an artifact of 19th century corporation law when par was suppose to represent the stock's value. Unscrupulous promoters used to sell stock with a $100 par value to strangers for $100 and sell the same stock to their friends for $1. As a result a law was passed that anyone who took stock directly from the issuing company for less than par was liable for the difference between their price and par should the company go bankrupt. Par is now set very low.

Additional Paid In Capital

The value of a company's stock may be far greater than its par value. The excess value the company receives over par is called Additional Paid In Capital. For example, a company may set par value at $1 per share, but sell 100,000 shares for $10 each. The total raised would be $1,000,000 which would be accounted for as follows. It would record Common Stock par value $1 and 100,000 shares issued $100,000; and Additional Paid in Capital $900,000.

Retained Earnings

Retained earnings are the company's accumulated net income since its inception less dividends paid. Other adjustments to retained earnings are minimal and rare for most companies.

Capital Stock In Treasury

Capital Stock in Treasury, usually called simply Treasury Stock, is stock that was once issued but has since been bought back by the company. Treasury stock reduces net equity. Reasons to repurchase a company's stock are to (i) have stock available to honor options, warrants, and conversion of preferred stock or bonds to common stock, (ii) have stock available for stock option plans, or (iii) reduce the number of shares outstanding so that remaining shareholders will own a greater share of the company's equity.

In the extreme, a controlling shareholder may have the company buy back so much stock that she or he ends up owning the company outright. The benefit of buying Treasury stock is that outstanding shares are purchased with the company's money and not the controlling shareholder's money.

Accumulated Other Comprehensive Income (Loss)

Accumulated other comprehensive income is used to adjust for things like gain or loss on foreign currency translation. These adjustments are non-operating which means they are unrelated to income from providing goods and services and they generally don't reflect gain or loss on sale of assets. Some view these adjustments as somewhat theoretical.

Total Liabilities and Shareholders Equity

This is an important total because it tests whether a company's books are in balance. The accounting equation requires Assets to equal Liabilities plus Equity. If the accounting equation is maintained Total Liabilities and Shareholders Equity will equal Total Assets. If it does not, there is a mistake somewhere in the financial statements.

Statement of Cash Flows

The purposes of the Statement of Cash Flows are to show where a company's cash came from, where it went, and to reconcile cash at the end of one year to cash at the end of the next year. Table 1-6 is a simplified Statement of Cash Flows. The Change in Cash is the net cash flow for the year. Cash at Beginning of Year is the cash on the prior year-end Balance Sheet. Cash at End of Year is the cash on the current year Balance Sheet. If all financial statements have been properly prepared, Change in Cash plus Cash at Beginning of Year should equal Cash at End of Year. Table 1-7 Campbell Soup Statement of Cash Flows 2007 is a more detailed version of the Statement of Cash Flows.

Table 1-6 Simplified Statement of Cash Flows

Cash Flow from Operations:
>   Net Income
>   Depreciation, Amortization and Non-Cash Expenses
>   Change in Accounts Receivable
>   Change in Inventory
>   Change in Accounts Payable
>   Changes in Other Working Capital Accounts
>   Adjustment for Gains or Losses on Sale of Assets
>>   Cash Flow from Operations

Cash Flow from Investing
>   Cash Outflows from Purchases of Investments and Plant, Property & Equipment
>   Cash Inflows from Sale of Investments and Plant, Property & Equipment
>>   Cash Flow from Investing

Cash Flow from Financing
>   Cash Inflow from Sale of Bonds, Loans and Other Borrowing
>   Cash Outflow from Redemption of Bonds and Repayment of Loans
>   Cash Outflow for Dividend Payments
>   Cash Inflow from Sale of Company Stock
>   Cash Outflow from Purchase of Company Stock
>>   Cash Flows from Financing Activities

Reconciliation
>   Change in Cash
>   Cash at the Beginning of Year
>   Cash at the End of the Year

Net Income

Net Income is the result of selling goods and services less expenses associated with operations, financing and taxes. Net Income generates cash. Net losses use cash.

Table 1-7 Campbell Soup Statement of Cash Flows 2007
(Dollars in Millions)

	2007	2006	2005
Cash Flows from Operations:			
Net earnings	$ 854	$ 766	707
Change in accounting method (Note 13)	—	(8)	—
Stock-based compensation	83	85	28
Resolution of tax matters (Note 8)	(25)	(60)	—
Reversal of legal reserves	(20)	—	—
Depreciation and amortization	283	289	279
Deferred taxes	10	29	47
Gain on sale of businesses (Note 3)	(42)	—	—
Gain on sale of facility	(23)	—	—
Other, net (Note 13)	61	82	81
Changes in working capital			
Accounts receivable	(68)	(18)	(10)
Inventories	(29)	(2)	21
Prepaid assets	(3)	—	(17)
Accounts payable and accrued liabilities	(128)	168	(26)
Pension fund contributions	(32)	(52)	(61)
Payments for hedging activities	(186)	(9)	(19)
Other (Note 13)	(61)	(44)	(40)
Cash Provided by Operations	674	1,226	990
Cash Flows from Investing:			
Purchases of plant assets	(334)	(309)	(332)
Sales of plant assets	23	2	11
Sales of businesses, net of cash divested (Note 3)	906	—	—
Other, net	8	13	7
Cash Flows from Investing:	603	(294)	(314)
Cash from Financing Activities:			
Long-term borrowings (repayments)	(62)	202	—
Repayments of notes payable	(600)	—	—
Net short-term borrowings (repayments)	57	31	(354)
Dividends paid	(308)	(292)	(275)
Treasury stock purchases	(1,140)	(506)	(110)
Treasury stock issuances	165	236	71
Excess tax benefits on stock-based compensation	25	11	—
Cash from Financing Activities	(1,863)	(318)	(668)
Exchange Rate Change Effects	—	3	—
Change in Cash	(586)	617	8
Cash — Beginning of Period	657	40	32
Cash — End of Period	$ 71	$ 657	$ 40

Cash Flows from Operations is cash generated in the normal course of business.

Cash Flows from Operations includes net income plus non-cash expenses and adjustments for sale of assets not in the ordinary course of business.

Working capital accounts are balance sheet accounts that rise and fall because of normal business operations and related adjustments.

Cash from Operations is the net effect of generating and using cash in operations and changes in working capital accounts.

Cash Flows from Investing summarizes cash used and generated from purchase and sale of plant, property and equipment, land, businesses, and the stocks and bonds of other companies.

Cash from Financing Activities includes cash generated issuing stock and bonds, and taking out loans. Uses of cash include repurchase of a company's own stock (Treasury stock), payoff of bonds, and loans and dividends.

Sometimes exchange rates on foreign assets affect cash used.

The Change in Cash plus Cash at the Beginning of Period should equal Cash at the End of Period otherwise there is an error in one of the financial statements.

Depreciation, Amortization, and other Non-Cash Expenses

Not every expense deducted from sales uses cash. When a company purchases raw materials it writes checks, when it hires and uses labor it writes checks, when it rents a factory or office building it writes checks, when it uses electricity, water or pays its taxes, it writes checks. Who does a company write checks to for depreciation and amortization? No one. Depreciation and amortization are expenses, but they are non-cash expenses.

If a company buys a truck for $60,000, uses it for five years and sells it for $10,000 it has used up $50,000 of the truck's value. One fifth of the value used up will be subtracted from sales as depreciation expense each year. Depreciation is a non-cash expense. The reduction of patent's value or leasehold improvements over time are also non-cash expenses called amortization. Since depreciation and amortization do not use cash, they must be added back to net income to get a more accurate understanding of the cash generated by operations.

Changes in Accounts Receivable

When a company sells on credit, it is lending money to its customers as surely as if it were handing them a check. This is a use of cash. Collecting from customers is a source of cash. In most companies selling on credit and collecting happen continuously. The issue is whether the company is lending money faster than it is collecting, or whether it is collecting faster than it is lending. If it is lending money faster than it is collecting there is a net use of cash. Stated differently, if this year's accounts receivable is higher than last year's accounts receivable, the difference is the net use of cash. Of course it is possible for collections to exceed credit sales. In that case accounts receivable will decline year over year. The net reduction in accounts receivable is a source of cash.

Changes in Inventory

Purchasing inventory uses cash, selling inventory is a source of cash. If inventory is purchased faster than it is sold, inventory will rise year over year. The year over year increase in inventory is a net use of cash. However, if inventory is sold faster than it is purchased, and inventory declines, the year over year reduction in inventory is a source of cash.

Changes in Accounts Payable

When a company buys on credit, its supplier is lending it cash as surly as if it handed the company a check. When a company pays its bills, it is using cash. If it is borrowing cash faster than it is using cash, accounts payable will increase year over year. The net increase in accounts payable is a source of cash. However, if a company pays off its bills faster than it incurs new ones, the decrease in accounts payable is a net use of cash.

Changes in Working Capital Accounts

Working capital is defined as current assets less current liabilities. The name working capital is derived from the fact that these accounts change all the time during the course of business operations. Examples of current assets are cash, accounts receivable, inventory and pre-paid expenses. Examples of current liabilities include accounts payable and accrued payroll.

In developing Cash from Operations, the three most important year to year balance sheet changes are for Accounts Receivable, Inventory and Accounts Payable. Most companies have these accounts. Companies can have other working capital accounts and changes in those accounts must be considered for the statement of cash flows to balance.

Change in Accounting Method

A change in accounting method can change net income which can change cash flows. For example, a company might change its method of depreciation, which would change its net income, or it might change the way it values inventory. The exact nature of the change should be explained in footnotes to financial statements. Changes in accounting method should be rare and few Statements of Cash Flow will have a line item like this.

Stock Based Compensation

If stock or options are awarded to an employee, the award may not result in an immediate cash outflow, but may result in a non-cash expense. Suppose a company's stock is valued at $20 per share and the company awards options with a strike price (a guaranteed price at which stock can be purchased) of $22 per share. Under GAAP an expense must be booked for those options. In effect, the GAAP mandated expense anticipates the company's stock price will rise above $22 at the some time. Not every company awards stock based compensation.

Resolution of Tax Matters

To say taxes are complex is an understatement. A significant problem for financial reporting is that a company and the IRS or state taxing authorities may disagree over the amount of tax due and owing. The income statement reports the amount of tax a company reasonably believes it owes. Years later, a company may have to make additional tax payments to resolve a dispute. On the other hand, sometimes the tax payer overpays and is entitled to a refund once disputes with taxing authorities are resolved. Not every company has a disputed tax matter that is so material (significant) that it is reported as a separate line item on the Statement of Cash Flows.

Reversal of Legal Reserves

If a company thinks it may lose a case or have significant legal bills on a case, it might book an expense for anticipated losses. At the point in time it incurs the loss, it does not pay anything. Instead, it sets up a liability account called a "reserve." Since it doesn't pay anything, this is a non-cash expense which should be added back to income to get cash flows from operations. Now suppose the company set up a "reserve" that was too big or it won its case. It would have to reverse everything. Where a non-cash expense must be added, reversal of a non-cash expenses must be subtracted from operating cash. Few companies have litigation reserves reported as a separate line item on the Statement of Cash Flows.

Deferred Taxes

Most companies keep one set of books for financial reporting and one set of books for taxes because GAAP and tax accounting rules are different. When income tax for financial reporting purposes is greater than taxes for income tax purposes, a non-cash expense is created. Suppose the tax on income per GAAP standards is $100,000, but because of timing differences due to using accelerated for the tax books, the actual tax payable is only $80,000. Of the $100,000 tax expense recorded on financial statements, $20,000 is a non-cash expense. All non-cash expenses must be added back to net income to accurately reflect cash from operations.

Prepaid Tax

Sometimes the tax payable under IRS rules is greater than the tax recorded on financial statements because of timing differences. If a company pays $100,000 in taxes, but only records $80,000 on its financial statements, it will have Prepaid tax of $20,000. A company will either have Prepaid or Deferred tax, but not both.

Gain on Sale of Assets, Facilities and Businesses

The second section of the Statement of Cash Flows reports cash used when assets are purchased; and cash generated when assets are sold. This is different from the Income Statement which reports the gain or loss on sale of assets.

Suppose a company has a business with a basis (cost less depreciation and amortization) of $12 million. If it sells that business for $20 million in cash, it will have a gain of $8 million reported on the Income Statement and that will become part of net income, the first item in Cash Flow From Operations. If $20 million in cash is reported in Cash Flow From Investing, the portion of the sale represented by the gain will be double counted. To avoid double counting, gains on sales of items reported in Cash Flow From Investing are subtracted from Cash Flow From Operations. The same logic applies to sale of assets like trucks or factories.

Other Net

Other can include such a broad variety of adjustments to cash flow that it would be impossible to characterize. The Other category usually represents a small fraction of cash flow items and footnotes should provide more detail.

Pre-Paid Assets

Pre-paid assets are bills paid in advance. The rational for calling pre-paid bills assets is that they will help a company generate income over future periods. Examples of pre-paid assets include pre-paid rent and insurance. For example on December 28, a company pays for an insurance policy that will run from January 1 to December 31 of the next year. On January 31st of the next year, one month's worth of the insurance will be used up. The used up value of that insurance will be booked as an expense and the value of pre-paid insurance will be reduced. A year to year increase in prepaid assets is a use of cash, a year over year decrease in prepaid assets is a source of cash.

Accrued Liabilities

Accrued liabilities are money owed to suppliers even though a supplier has not yet sent a bill. Aluminum smelters use a lot of electricity. Even though an electric company may send bills on the 15th of the month, the smelter must book as an expense the electricity used between the last bill and month end. Accrued liabilities are often based on estimates like meter readings. Increasing accrued liabilities is a source of cash since suppliers are providing something that has not yet been paid for; decreasing accrued liabilities is a use of cash.

Pension Fund Contributions

Pension fund accounting is complex and beyond the scope of this book. As a general rule, pension fund contributions are money set aside to pay defined retirement benefits. Actuarial assumptions, return on plan assets and other factors make contribution calculations complex and results highly volatile. Most companies with defined benefit plans explain contribution calculations in footnotes. Many large companies are terminating their defined benefit plans. Contributions are a use of cash.

Payments for Hedging Activities

Hedging has to do with buying or selling contracts that lock in the price of goods to be delivered in the future. There is a sound reason for companies to lock in the cost of an input early if one thinks the price will rise, or a good reason for farmers to lock in the price at which they can sell their harvest. Hedging has spread far beyond locking in the price of goods for future delivery. Companies with no interest in owning a particular good buy and sell contracts to exploit anticipated price moves. A complete description of hedging is beyond the scope of this book. The nature of the hedging done by a company should be disclosed in the notes to financial statements.

Cash Flows From Investing

Intuitively one might think of cash flows from investing as buying and selling stocks and bonds. But, cash flow from investing in a Statement of Cash Flows includes purchase of plant, equipment, furnishings and fixtures, patents, copyrights, land, as well as stocks and bonds of other companies. Purchase of these items is a use of cash. Purchase of supplies or inventory is not investing.

Investing also includes proceeds from sale of plant, equipment, furnishings and fixtures, patents, copyrights, land, as well as stocks and bonds of other companies. Sale of assets is a source of cash. Sales included in Cash Flow From Operations are sales in the ordinary course of business; for example a baker selling bread. Sales included in Cash Flows From Investing are those that are not in the ordinary course of business, for example if a baker sells her ovens or one of her stores.

Cash Flows From Financing Activities

Financing activities are those activities needed to maintain a company's capital base. Capital can be either debt or equity. Issuing stock to investors is a financing activity that generates cash. Paying dividends is a use of cash. Issuing bonds generates cash, paying off bonds when they mature, or making contributions to a sinking fund are uses of cash. Borrowing money is a source of cash. Repayment of the principal part of a loan is a use of cash. Loan interest is captured as part of Net Income.

When a company repurchases its own stock, the repurchased stock is called Treasury Stock. A company can either retire this stock or it can re-issue it. Repurchase of a company's own stock uses cash. Re-issuance of Treasury stock generates cash.

When a company compensates employees with stock it creates an expense that reduces both net income and taxable income; which can reduce the cash outlay for taxes. This can give rise to an excess tax benefits on stock-based compensation. This is somewhat unusual adjustment in the Statement of Cash Flow and not many companies have this. The accounting and tax law behind this adjustment are beyond the scope of this book. If a company has an adjustment like this read the notes to the financial statement for more details.

Exchange Rate Effects

Companies with international operations may report fluctuations in the relative value of currency among counties. Sometimes these exchange rate effects impact the reconciliation of cash flow. The line item Exchange Rate Effects is relatively rare in a Statement of Cash Flows. If a company being analyzed has such a line item it usually provides details in a note to financial statements.

Change In Cash

The change in cash is the sum of Cash Flows from Operations, plus Cash Flows from Investing, plus Cash Flows from Financing Activities, plus Exchange Rate Effects. In the case of Campbell Soup for 2007, the Change in Cash was -$586 ($674 + $603 - $1,863 + $0).

Cash – Beginning of Period

The cash at the beginning of the period should be the same as the cash on the Balance Sheet at the end of the prior year.

Cash – End of Period

Cash at the end of the period should be the cash on the Balance Sheet at the end of the current year. Change in Cash plus Cash – at the Beginning of Period should equal Cash – at the End of Period, otherwise there is an error in the financial statements.

Conclusion

Generally Accepted Accounting Principals (GAAP) is based on accrual accounting in which revenue is booked when earned rather than when cash is received and expenses are recognized when incurred rather than when paid. GAAP requires four financial statements (i) the Income Statement, (ii) Statement of Retained Earnings, (iii) Balance Sheet and (iv) the Statement of Cash Flows. The Statement of Retained Earnings is rarely used to compute ratios and not discussed in this book. GAAP also requires notes to further clarify financial statements.

GAAP allows a great deal of flexibility in preparing financial statements. GAAP also allows a company to select the level of detail it uses for reporting. To make statements comparable from year to year and company to company, they should be recast into a standard format.

Within each financial statement there are certain landmarks. Identification of these landmarks aids analysis and helps keep one from getting bogged down in minutia. Landmarks in the Income Statement include revenue or sales, cost of goods sold, gross profit, overhead, selling and marketing expenses, other overhead, EBIT, interest net, EBT, taxes and Net Income. Landmarks within the Balance Sheet include current assets, current liabilities, total assets, total liabilities, equity and total liabilities plus equity. Landmarks in the Statement of Cash Flows include cash flow from operations, cash flow from investing, cash flow from financing and the reconciliation of cash year to year.

Financial statements are relatively easy to read if one focuses on finding the key landmarks in each statement and reads the notes accompanying financial statements. One need not be a trained accountant to understand what is going on.

CHAPTER 2 # Profitability

Introduction

Profitability is an accrual accounting concept. Accrual accounting recognizes revenue when it is earned and expenses when incurred. It has little to do with the receipt and disbursement of cash. As such, profitability is a somewhat artificial construct. Nevertheless, profitability is accepted as the best indicator of business success. This chapter will explore a set of ratios that contribute to, and measure profitability.

Sales Growth

Grow or die is the immutable law of business so a business that is not growing is already beginning to die. Annual sales growth is given by equation (2.1).

$$\text{Sales Growth} = \frac{\text{Sales}_2 - \text{Sales}_1}{\text{Sales}_1} \tag{2.1}$$

Where Sales_2 is the current year's sales and Sales_1 is prior year's sales. Sales Growth is always stated as a percent.

Suppose a company has sales of $20 million this year and sales of $18 million last year. What is its year to year sales growth?

$$\text{Sales Growth} = \frac{\$20 \text{ million} - \$18 \text{ million}}{\$18 \text{ million}}$$

$$= \$2 \text{ million} / \$18 \text{ million}$$

$$= 11.1\%$$

Compound Annual Sales Growth

Sales growth considers one year. Compound Annual Sales Growth, shown in equation (2.2) evens out growth over a number of years.

$$g = ((Sn / Sm)^{(1/(n-m))}) - 1 \tag{2.2}$$

Where g is the compound annual growth rate of sales; S_n is sales for the most current year and S_m is sales for the base year from which sales growth is measured. Note that the ratio of current year sales to base year sales is raised to a fractional power. The fractional power is one over the number of years between the base year and current year.

Suppose a company had $20 million in sales in 2010 and $11 million in sales in 2007. What is its compound annual growth rate?

$g = (($20 \text{ million} / $11 \text{ million})^{(1/(2010-2007))}) - 1$

$= (1.818)^{(1/3)} - 1$

$= (1.22) - 1$

$= 22.0\%$

Sales growth is always stated as a percentage.

COGS%

Cost of goods sold (COGS) is the cost to make the company's product, or to purchase the product, if the company is a retailer or wholesaler. For a service company, like a law firm, accounting firm, consulting firm, or temp agency, this is called the cost of services. Anything that doesn't directly go to making or buying products for resale or delivering a service is <u>excluded</u> from COGS. COG%, the percent of every dollar of sales consumed by COGS, is shown as equation (2.3). COGS% is important because COGS is usually the largest expense in any company.

COGS%= COGS / Sales   (2.3)

Suppose a company has $20 million in sales and its cost of goods sold is $13 million. What is its COGS%?

= $13 million / $20 million.

= 65%

COGS% is always stated as a percentage. If a company's COGS% is higher than its competitors or it is creeping up over time, that is a danger sign.

Gross Profit

Gross Profit is the difference between sales and cost of goods sold. It is what is left over after the product has been produced or service rendered as shown in equation (2.4). While Gross Profit is not strictly speaking a ratio, it is an important landmark in a financial statement.

Gross Profit= Sales – COGS   (2.4)

Suppose a company has $20 million in sales and its cost of goods sold is $13 million. What is its Gross Profit?

= $20 million - $13 million

= $7 million

Gross Profit is always quoted in dollars. Gross Profit must cover overhead, financing costs, taxes and profit.

Gross Margin

Gross Margin is the percent of every dollar of sales that is left over after the product has been made or service rendered. Gross margin must cover overhead, financing costs, taxes and profits. If gross margins get too thin a company will collapse. The equation for Gross Margin is (2.5).

$$\text{Gross Margin} = \frac{\text{Sales} - \text{COGS}}{\text{Sales}} \qquad (2.5)$$

Suppose a company has sales of $20 million and COGS of $13 million. What is its Gross Margin?

$$= \frac{\$20 \text{ million} - \$13 \text{ million}}{\$20 \text{ million}}$$

= 35%

Gross Margin is always stated as a percent. The sum of COGS% and Gross Margin must add up to 100%.

Overhead%

Overhead is a great killer of companies so it is important to closely monitor the percentage of sales needed to cover overhead. For purposes of this ratio, Overhead is defined as everything on an income statement between Gross Profit and Earnings Before Interest and Taxes. The formula for Overhead% is given in equation (2.6).

$$\text{Overhead\%} = \text{Overhead} / \text{Sales} \qquad (2.6)$$

Suppose a company has sales of $20 million and overhead of $4 million. What is Overhead%?

= $4 million / $ 20 million

= 20.0%

Overhead% is always stated as a percent. Overhead expenses should never grow faster than sales. If sales are growing faster than overhead then Overhead% should decline over time. If Overhead% is rising over time this is a sign of trouble.

Selling Cost%

The more precision with which one can measure performance, the better one can control it. Overhead can be subdivided into Selling and Marketing Expenses on the one hand, and Other Overhead on the other. The rational for subdividing Overhead is that one might reasonably expect Selling and Marketing Costs such as advertising, commissions and sales related travel to rise and fall with sales. However, Other Overhead should decline as sales rise. The formula for Selling Cost% is given by equation (2.7).

$$\text{Selling Cost\%} = \frac{\text{Selling and Marketing Expenses}}{\text{Sales}} \qquad (2.7)$$

Suppose a company has Sales of $20 million and Selling and Marketing Expenses of $1.2 million. What is its Selling Cost%?

$$= \$1.2 \text{ million} / \$20 \text{ million}$$

$$= 6.0\%$$

Selling Cost% is always reported as a percent. Not every company reports its Selling and Marketing Expenses. That doesn't mean this ratio is useless. It just means a company might not be able to compare its ratio to those of its competitors. It can still compare its Selling Cost% to its historical record.

Other Overhead%

Other Overhead is what is left of Overhead after Selling and Marketing Expenses have been removed. Since Other Overhead is not used to make or sell the product it deserves special scrutiny. Other Overhead% can be computed using equation (2.8).

$$\text{Other Overhead\%} = \frac{\text{Overhead} - \text{Selling and Marketing Expenses}}{\text{Sales}} \qquad (2.8)$$

Suppose a company has $20 million of sales, $4 million of Overhead and $1.2 million of Selling and Marketing Expenses. What is its Other Overhead%?

$$= \frac{\$4 \text{ million} - \$1.2 \text{ million}}{\$20 \text{ million}}$$

$$= 14.0\%$$

Other Overhead% is always stated as a percent. Other Overhead% should decline with increasing sales.

EBITDA Growth

EBITDA is Earnings before Interest and Taxes from the Income Statement plus Depreciation and Amortization from the Statement of Cash Flows. It is a rough estimate of the amount of cash generated by company operations. Whether EBITDA is growing or declining over time will determine whether and how successful a company will be. The year over year change in EBITDA can be calculated using equation (2.9).

$$\text{EBITDA Growth} = (EBITDA_2 - EBIDDA_1) / EBITDA_1 \qquad (2.9)$$

Where $EBITDA_2$ is the most recent year and $EBITDA_1$ is the prior year. Suppose a company had an EBITDA of $12 million this year, $11 million last year. What is its year over year EBITDA growth?

$$= \$(12M - \$11M) / \$11M$$

$$= 9.1\%$$

Compound annual EBITDA growth, calculated using equation (2.10), provides a broader picture of a company's performance by considering growth rates over several years.

$$\text{Compound Annual EBITDA Growth} = (((EBITDA_n / EBITDA_m))^{((1/(n-m))}) - 1 \qquad (2.10)$$

$EBITDA_n$ is the most recent EBITDA and $EBITDA_m$ is the year chosen as the starting point for measurement. The expression in the exponent (n-m) the number of years over which the measurement is taking place. Suppose a company had an EBITDA of $12 million in 2010, and $7 million in 2005. What is its compound annual EBITDA growth?

$$= (\$12M / \$7M)^{(1/(2010-2005))} - 1$$

$$= (\$12M / \$7M)^{(1/5)} - 1$$

$$= (1.714)^2 - 1$$

$$= 1.1138 - 1$$

$$= .1138 = 11.38\%$$

EBITDA Growth is always stated as a percentage.

Interest Burden

Many companies get crushed under a burden of debt. One indicator of whether a company is edging toward trouble is the percentage of sales consumed by interest expense. Interest Burden can be computed using equation (2.11).

Interest Burden= Interest Expense net/Sales (2.11)

Interest Burden is always quoted as a percentage. Suppose a company had sales of $20 million, interest expense of $1.5 million and interest income is $0.3 million. What is the Interest Burden?

= ($1.5 million - $0.3 million) / $20 million

= $1.2 million / $20 million

= 6%

Effective Tax Rate

A company's effective tax rate might be far different than the rate published in the Internal Revenue Code because of penalties, credits and timing differences. A company's effective tax rate is a company's Tax Expense divided by Earnings Before Taxes (EBT) as shown in equation (2.12).

Tax Rate= Tax Expense/Earnings Before Taxes (2.12)

Suppose a company has EBT of $2 million and tax expense of $0.6 million. What is its effective tax rate?

= $0.6 million/$2 million

= 30%

Tax rates are always quoted as percentage.

Profit Margin

Profit Margin is used to determine how efficiently a company converts sales into net income. Some companies use a lot of debt, some use little, some use none at all. To make companies comparable, the effect of various debt levels must be adjusted out. In effect, we want to compare company operations independent of debt load. To do this we add after tax net interest expense back to net income. Net interest is interest expense less interest income.

Interest is tax deductible, which means $100 of interest paid to a bank does not decrease net income by $100. If a company's tax rate is 30%, that $100 deduction will reduce taxable income by $100 and save the company $30 ($100 x 30%). The after tax cost of the interest is only $70 ($100 - $30). The formula for Profit Margin is given by equation (2.13).

$$\text{Profit Margin} = \frac{\text{Net Income} + \text{Interest (net)} \times (1 - \text{Tax Rate})}{\text{Sales}} \qquad (2.13)$$

Suppose a company had Sales of $20 million, Net Income of $1.5 million, Interest Expense of $1.7 million, Interest Income of $0.2 million, and it was in the 30% tax bracket. What would its Profit Margin be?

$$= \frac{\$1.5 \text{ million} + (\$1.7 \text{ million} - \$0.2 \text{ million}) \times (1 - 30\%)}{\$20 \text{ million}}$$

$$= \frac{\$1.5 \text{ million} + \$1.5 \text{ million} \times 70\%}{\$20 \text{ million}}$$

$$= \$2.55 \text{ million} / \$20 \text{ million}$$

$$= 12.75\%$$

Profit Margin is always stated as a percent. If a company has discontinued operations or extraordinary items, one might want to use earnings from continuing operations rather than net income in equation (2.13)

Earnings per Share

Most people don't buy companies, they buy shares of stock in companies. Many companies have preferred as well as common stock, but preferred stock is generally not available to the public. Preferred dividends have the first claim on earnings. The remaining earnings can be attributed to common stock. The formula for Earnings per Share (EPS) is given by equation (2.14).

$$\text{EPS} = \frac{\text{Net Income} - \text{Preferred Dividends}}{\text{Weighted Average Common Shares Outstanding}} \qquad (2.14)$$

The weighted average common shares outstanding is usually reported at the end of the income statement. EPS is reported as dollars per share.

Suppose a company has $1.5 million of Net Income, $0.2 million of preferred dividends, and 3.0 million shares of common stock outstanding. What is its EPS?

$$= \frac{\$1.5 \text{ million} - \$0.2 \text{ million}}{3.0 \text{ million}}$$

$$= \$1.3 \text{ million} / 3.0 \text{ million}$$

$$= \$0.43 \text{ per share}$$

Weighted Average Shares Outstanding

Assets, accounts receivable, inventory and even retained earnings tend to grow or shrink fairly evenly over the course of a year, so an average of the beginning and ending values is usually a reasonable estimate of annual value. However, stocks tend to get issued, split or repurchased on specific dates. If that date is toward the beginning or the end of a year, a simple average will not provide a realistic picture of the number of outstanding shares. A weighted average, as shown in equation (2.15) provides a much truer picture.

$$\text{Weighted Average Shares} = \frac{\sum_1^n \text{Shares}_i \times \text{Time}_i}{\sum_1^n \text{Time}_i} \qquad (2.15)$$

Where Time_i is some interval of time, which can be measured in days, weeks or months and Shares_i are the number of shares outstanding over that interval. If there is a stock split, every share outstanding before the date of the split must be counted as many times as the shares split to be equivalent to one year-end share. If there is a reverse stock split during the year, each share prior to the split must be counted as a fraction of the year-end share.

Suppose a company has 4.0 million shares outstanding on January 1, it issues 1.0 million shares on May 1, it has a three to one stock split August 1, and issues 1.0 million shares on December 1. What is its weighted average number of shares?

There are four time intervals. The first runs from January 1 to April 30, or 4 months; the second runs from May 1 to July 31 or 3 months; the third interval runs from August 1 to November 30 or 4 months; and the fourth interval runs from December 1 to December 31 or 1 month. The company had 4.0 million shares outstanding for 4 months (January 1 to April 30) and 5.0 million shares outstanding for 3 months (May 1 to July 31). Then the stock split three to one. Once that happens, one must go back and adjust all the pre-split shares to make them equivalent to post split shares.

The equivalent post-split shares outstanding January 1 to April 30, is now 12.0 million (4.0 million x 3). The post-split equivalent shares outstanding May 1 to July 31 is 15.0 million (5.0 million x 3). Over the interval August 1 to November 30 the number of post-split shares does not change and remains constant at 15.0 million shares. On December 1, 1.0 million post-split shares are added for a total of 16.0 million shares outstanding for one month.

$$\text{Weighted Average Shares} = \frac{12.0 \times 4 \text{ mo.} + 15.0 \times 3 \text{ mo.} + 15.0 \times 4 \text{ mo.} + 16.0 \times 1 \text{ mo.}}{4 \text{ mo.} + 3 \text{ mo.} + 4 \text{ mo.} + 1 \text{ mo.}}$$

$$= \frac{48.0 + 45.0 + 60.0 + 16.0}{12.0}$$

= 169.0 / 12.0

= 14.08 million shares outstanding

Weighted average shares outstanding is always measured in number of shares regardless of how the time interval is measured. Because this calculation is somewhat tedious, it is prone to errors. Therefore, one should always ask whether the answer is reasonable. A reasonable weighted average would be greater than the lowest number of post-split equivalent shares, in this case 12.0 million, and less than the maximum number of post-split adjusted shares, in this case 16.0 million. The answer of 14.08 million shares seems reasonable on this basis.

Price Earnings Ratio

The price earnings ratio (PE) ratio is the stock's current price divided by its last EPS. Sophisticated analysts sometimes compute their own EPS based on a rolling four quarters of statements. It's unclear whether this is better because quarterly data do not usually have all the refinements of year end data. One might think of the PE ratio as the number of dollars it takes to purchase one dollar of a company's earnings.

If a company's historical PE ratio is 16, and because of fluctuations in stock price it has a PE ratio of 12 on a particular day, some analysts see this is a buying opportunity because the market is temporarily undervaluing the stock. If a company's historical PE is 16 and because of stock price fluctuations, its PE is 22 on a given day, some analysts see this as a selling opportunity because the market is temporarily overvaluing the stock. Not all analysts agree that changes in a PE ratio signal buying and selling opportunities. The formula for PE ratio is given by equation (2.16).

PE Ratio= Stock Price / EPS   (2.16)

Suppose a company has an EPS of $.50 and the stock price on a given day is $9.00. What is its PE Ratio?

= $9.00 / $0.50

= 18

The PE ratio is a dimensionless number.

Return on Equity

Return on Equity (ROE), also called Return on Common Equity (ROCE) is the return that common shareholders get on average equity. Since Preferred Shareholders take earnings first, preferred dividends are subtracted from net income before common shareholders measure returns.

If no shares have been issued or repurchased, and there have been no substantial dividend payments, average equity can be estimated as the equity at the end of the year plus equity at the end of the prior year divided by two. The formula for ROE under these circumstances is given by equation (2.17)

$$\text{ROE} = \frac{\text{Net Income} - \text{Preferred Dividends}}{(\text{Equity}_2 + \text{Equity}_1) / 2} \qquad (2.17)$$

Where Equity_2 and Equity_1 are the equity in the company at the end of the current and prior year respectively. Suppose a company has $1.5 million of net income, $0.2 million of preferred dividends, equity at the end of the current year is $11 million and at the end of the prior year was $10 million. What is its ROE?

$$= \frac{\$1.5 \text{ million} - \$0.2 \text{ million}}{(\$11 \text{ million} + \$10 \text{ million}) / 2}$$

$$= \$1.3 \text{ million} / \$10.5 \text{ million}$$

$$= 12.4\%$$

Return on Equity is always stated as a percentage.

Payout Ratio

Corporations can elect to reinvest some or all of their profits in the company. On the other hand, the prospect of receiving dividends encourages many to invest in stocks. Most companies that pay dividends have a policy as to the amount of net income they pay out. This is known as the Payout Ratio, and is show in equation (2.18).

$$\text{Payout Ratio} = \text{Cash Dividends} / \text{Net Income} \qquad (2.18)$$

Suppose a company has net income of $7.5 million and pays its common shareholders $1.5 million. What is its Payout Ratio?

$$= \$1.5 \text{ million} / \$7.5 \text{ million}$$

$$= 20\%$$

The Payout Ratio is always quoted as a percent.

Book Value per Share

Book Value is thought by many to place a minimum value on a company's stock. Book Value is a company's assets, less its liabilities. In other words, book value is net equity. Book Value per Share is a company's equity divided by the number of outstanding shares at year end. Book Value per Share can then be compared to a stock's market value. Market values are subject to many forces, trends and factors that have nothing to do with the underlying value of a company. One might find the market price of a share is less than its book value per share. Some argue this represents a buying opportunity. Book Value per Share can be computed using equation (2.19).

$$\text{Book Value per Share} = \frac{\text{Equity}}{\text{Year end shares outstanding}} \qquad (2.19)$$

Suppose a company has equity of $4.0 million and 1.25 million shares outstanding.

= $4.0 million / 1.25 million shares

= $3.20 per share

Dividend Yield

Many, but not all stocks, pay dividends. The dividend yield is the last annual common stock dividend, divided by its current stock price as shown in equation (2.20).

Dividend Yield= Common Dividend / Stock Price   (2.20)

Suppose a stock paid a common dividend of $0.27 per share and the current stock price is $9.00. What is the dividend yield?

= $0.27 / $9.00

= 3.0%

Dividend yield is always stated as a percent.

Total Yield

When people buy stocks they purchase them for growth or dividends or both. Total yield takes the growth of a stock's earnings and value into account when determining the total yield. If the relationship among COGS%, Overhead% and other expenses to sales remains the same and the PE ratio remains about the same, then sales growth can be used to estimate growth in the total yield as shown in equation (2.21).

Total Yield = (Dividends / Price) + growth   (2.21)

Here growth is the compound annual growth rate computed above. Suppose a company has annual dividends of $0.27, a stock price of $9.00 and a growth rate of 22% per year. What is its Total Yield?

= ($.27 / $9.00) + 22%

= 3% + 22%

= 25%

Total Yield is always expressed as a percentage.

Conclusion

The concept of profitability is based on accrual accounting which says revenue may only be recorded when it is earned, not when cash is received and expenses are recorded when incurred, not when cash is expended. As such, this makes the concept of profitability somewhat artificial. Nevertheless it is still considered one of the best measures of company performance.

Profitability is the result of a long series of actions and events, all of which must be trending in the correct direction for a company to stay profitable. Sales must grow; the cost of goods sold as a percentage of sales must remain steady or decline, overhead as a percentage of sales should decline as sales increase, and the burden of interest expense should not be too great.

Since most people buy shares of stock rather than whole companies, a number of measures of value have been developed at the shareholder level including earnings per share, return on common equity, payout ratio, dividend yield and total stock yield.

Companies never switch from profitable to unprofitable or unprofitable to profitable overnight. Ratio trends can help identify companies on the right track and those on the point of collapse.

CHAPTER 3

Cash Flow

Introduction

Cash is a company's life blood. If a company runs out of cash it won't be able to meet payroll and other obligations, and it will die. Generating cash is different than making a profit. A company can be profitable and run out of cash or a company can generate cash but show no profit.

Cash Flow – Simple

A simple method of estimating cash flow is to add non-cash expenses to net income. Non-cash expenses are accounting expenses that don't require cash expenditures. When a company has expenses for rent, utilities, payroll or raw materials it has to write checks and expend cash. However, expenses like depreciation and amortization do not result in cash expenditures. So to estimate cash flow from operations non-cash expenditures like depreciation and amortization must be added back as shown in equation (3.1)

$$\text{Cash Flow Simple} = \text{Net Income} + \text{Depreciation} + \text{Amortization} \qquad (3.1)$$

Suppose a company has net income of $600 million, depreciation of $80 million and amortization of $20 million.

$$= \$600 \text{ million} + \$80 \text{ million} + \$20 \text{ million}$$

$$= \$700 \text{ million}$$

Cash Flow Simple has been criticized because it doesn't take into account cash which must be reinvested in accounts receivable, inventory, plant and equipment to grow a business.

Cash Flow – Complex a.k.a. Free Cash Flow

In the real world, companies must constantly re-invest cash to grow. That means cash flow simple overestimates the cash available to invest in new products, advertising campaigns, to acquire other companies or distribute to shareholders.

So what uses up a company's cash? Selling to customers on credit is like lending customers money and this uses cash. Collecting accounts receivable generates cash. If credit sales outpace collections, then accounts receivable will increase. The year to year increase in receivables represents the net use of cash. However, if accounts receivable decrease year over year, the net decrease is a source of cash.

Purchasing inventory uses cash. Selling inventory generates cash. If inventory increases year over year, there is a net use of cash. However, if inventory decreases, that is a source of cash. Purchasing plant, property and equipment (PP&E) uses cash. Selling PP&E is a source of cash.

When a supplier sells to a company on credit, the company is borrowing money which is a source of cash. When a company pays its suppliers it uses cash. If accounts payable increases from year to year, cash is generated. If accounts payable decreases year over year, cash is used.

Many companies pay dividends. Cash expended on dividends is not available for other corporate purposes and is a use of cash.

When all these adjustments are added together we can estimate Cash Flow Complex as shown in equation (3.2). Some call this free cash flow, which is cash that is free for any purpose a company desires.

$$
\begin{aligned}
\text{Cash Flow Complex} = \ &\text{Net Income} \\
&+ \text{Depreciation and amortization} \\
&- \text{Increase in accounts receivable} \\
&- \text{Increase in inventory} \\
&+ \text{Increase in accounts payable} \\
&- \text{Net Additions to PP\&E} \\
&- \text{Dividends}
\end{aligned}
\tag{3.2}
$$

This equation may be modified for a particular company if it uses cash or generates cash in a manner not discussed.

Net income can be found on the income statement. Balance sheets for two years are compared to determine whether accounts receivable, inventory, and accounts payable increase or decrease. Depreciation and amortization as well as the investment in PP&E can be found on the statement of cash flows.

Example: A company has net income of $600, depreciation of $80, amortization of $20, purchased $70 of PP&E and paid dividends of $150.

Balance Sheet		
Dollars in millions	2010	2009
Cash	$80	$50
Accounts Receivable	$700	$600
Inventory	$820	$700
PP&E	$1,020	$950
Total Assets	$2,620	$2,300
Accounts Payable	$500	$400
Bank Loans	$1.000	$900
Total Liabilities	$1,500	1,300
Total Equity	$1,120	$1,000
Total Liabilities & Equity	$2,620	$2,300

What is Cash Flow Complex?

Accounts receivable increased $100 (from $600 to $700) this used cash. Inventory increased $120 (from $700 to $820) this used cash. Accounts payable increased by $100 (from $400 to $500) this is a source of cash.

Cash Flow Complex = $600 + $80 +20 -$100 - $120 +$100 -$70 -$150

= $360

This compares to Cash Flow Simple of $700 ($600 + $80 + $20).

EBITDA

EBITDA is another important estimate of cash generated by a company's core operations. EBITDA is earnings before interest, taxes, depreciation and amortization. EBITDA is found by adding depreciation and amortization to earnings before interest and taxes (EBIT) as shown in equation (3.3).

$$EBITDA = EBIT + Depreciation + Amortization \qquad (3.3)$$

Companies vary in their financing and tax strategy. EBITDA provides a look at cash generated before financing and tax strategies come into play. EBITDA is used in company valuations.

Suppose a company has Earnings Before Interest and Tax (EBIT) of $1,200, depreciation of $80 and amortization of $20. What is its EBITDA?

= $1,200 + $80 +$20

= $1,300

EBITDA to Assets

The ratio EBITDA to Assets is a measure of the cash flow generated by each dollar of assets as shown in equation (3.4).

$$\text{EBITDA to Assets} = \frac{\text{EBIT} + \text{Depreciation \& Amortization}}{(\text{Assets}_2 + \text{Assets}_1)/2} \qquad (3.4)$$

Where Assets_2 are the assets at the end of the current year and Assets_1 are the assets at the end of the prior year.

Suppose a company has assets of \$2,500 and \$2,300 this year and last, EBIT of \$400, and depreciation and amortization of \$80 and \$20 respectively. What is EBITDA to Assets?

$$= \frac{\$400 + \$80 + \$20}{(\$2,500 + \$2,300)/2}$$

$$= \$500 / \$2,400$$

$$= 20.8\%$$

The ratio of EBITDA to Assets is always stated as a percentage.

EBITDA to Sales

The ratio EBITDA to Sales is a measure of how much cash is being generated from every dollar of sales, as shown in equation (3.5).

$$\text{EBITDA to Sales} = \frac{\text{EBIT} + \text{Depreciation} + \text{Amortization}}{\text{Sales}} \qquad (3.5)$$

Suppose a company has Sales of \$3,000, EBIT of \$400, and depreciation and amortization of \$80 and \$20 respectively. What is EBITDA to Sales?

$$= \frac{\$400 + \$80 + \$20}{\$3,000}$$

$$= \$500 / \$3000$$

$$= 16.7\%$$

The ratio EBITDA to Sales is always stated as a percentage.

Times Interest Earned

Times interest earned is a measure of whether a company is generating enough income to pay its interest expense. This ratio is particularly important to banks. The formula for Times Interest Earned is given by equation (3.6).

$$\text{Times Interest Earned} = \frac{\text{EBIT}}{\text{Interest Expense}} \tag{3.6}$$

Suppose a company has EBIT of $400 and interest expense of $80. What is Times Interest Earned?

= $400 / $80

= 5.0

Times Interest Earned is a dimensionless number. No bank will lend to a company with a Times Interest Earned Ratio of 1.0 or less because such a company is not generating enough pre-tax income to pay interest. Even a Times Interest Earned of 2.0 leaves little income to grow a company after making interest payments.

Debt Service Coverage

A criticism of Times Interest Earned is that it does not take into account principal on loan payments, bond sinking fund payments, payments on operating leases, the principal portion of capital leases, all of which are fixed obligations which must be funded from operations. The Debt Service Coverage ratio is given in equation (3.7).

$$\text{Debt Service Coverage} = \frac{\text{EBIT}}{\substack{\text{Interest Expense} + \text{Loan Principal} \\ + \text{Operating Lease Payments} \\ + \text{Capital Lease Payments} \\ + \text{Sinking Fund Payments}}} \tag{3.7}$$

Sinking fund payments are payments a company makes to a trust fund so that there will be enough set aside to redeem bond principal at maturity.

Suppose a company has EBIT of $400, interest expense of $80, loan principal payments of $70, operating lease payments of $10, capital lease payments of $20 and sinking fund payments of $30. What is its Debt Service Coverage Ratio?

$$= \frac{\$400}{\$80 + \$70 + \$10 + \$20 + \$30}$$

= $400 / $210

= 1.90

The Times Interest Earned ratio would seem to indicate a company would have no problem meeting its financing obligations. However, in this example, the Debt Service Coverage Ratio indicates the company isn't generating much income over and above what is needed for debt service.

Burn Rate

Most companies including troubled companies and start-ups generate some cash each month. When a company uses cash for operations faster than it generates cash from operations it has a burn rate as shown in equation (3.8).

Burn Rate= Cash Used in Operations – Cash Generated in Operations   (3.8)

A company's burn rate can be used to determine how fast it is using up its capital. It can be used to determine how long before a company is insolvent (no longer able to pay its bills) as shown in equation (3.9). Burn rate has no meaning if a company is generating more cash from operations than it uses for operations.

Time to Insolvency = Available Cash / Burn Rate   (3.9)

Suppose a company generates $5 million a month from operations, uses $7 million a month for operations and has $9 million in cash reserves. What is its burn rate and when will it run out of cash?

Burn Rate   = $7 million / month - $5 million / month

                       = $2 million / month

Time to Insolvency   = $9 million / $2 million / month

                       = 4.5 months

Taxes and Cash Flow

Tax strategy can have a dramatic impact on cash flow. Use of techniques like accelerated depreciation and other techniques beyond the scope of this book can be used to defer recognition of income for tax purposes. Even though most tax deferral strategies reverse over a period of years, real cash flow can be increased by legally delaying recognition of taxable income. Delaying recognition allows a company to pay its taxes with cheaper future dollars.

Equation (3.10) can be used to estimate the amount of savings by postponing payment of taxes.

$$\text{Tax Savings} = \text{Taxable Income} \times \text{Tax Rate} - \frac{\text{Taxable Income} \times \text{Tax Rate}}{(1 + K)^n} \qquad (3.10)$$

Suppose a company in the 30% tax bracket could recognize a taxable income of $100,000 now or defer it for five years. Further, suppose the company's cost of capital is 8%.

$$\text{Tax Savings}= \$100,000 \times 30\% - \frac{\$100,000 \times 30\%}{(1+8\%)^5}$$

$$= \$30,000 - \$30,000 / 1.469$$

$$= \$30,000 - \$20,422$$

$$= \$9,578$$

If this company recognized the taxable income immediately, it would have to pay $30,000 in taxes ($100,000 x 30%). However, if it was legally able to defer recognition of income for five years the tax cost in present dollars would only be $20,422 because of the time value of money ($100,000 x 30%) / ((1 +8%)^5). The difference is a savings in present dollars of $9,578.

Cash Flow per Share

Cash flow per share is the amount of cash allocable to one share of common stock. Cash flow per share effectively sets an upper limit on dividends. Estimate cash flow, then subtract preferred dividends because they are not available to common shareholders and divide the result by the number of outstanding shares as shown in equation 3.11.

$$\text{Cash Flow Per Share}= \frac{\text{Net Income +Depreciation + Amortization – Pref. Dividends}}{\text{Outstanding Shares}} \quad (3.11)$$

Suppose a company has net income of $600 million, depreciation of $80 million and amortization of $20 million, preferred stock dividends of $25 million and had 200 million shares outstanding. What is its Cash Flow per Share?

$$= \frac{\$600M + \$80M + \$20M - \$25M}{200M \text{ Shares}}$$

$$= \$675 M / 200M \text{ Shares}$$

$$= \$3.375 \text{ per share}$$

Conclusion

Cash represents a motive force for a company. Cash flow is necessary to pay a company's bills on a sustainable basis. Cash flow is also needed to grow a company.

There are many was to estimate a company's cash flow including cash flow simple which is net income plus depreciation and amortization, and free cash flow which takes into account cash that must be reinvested in a company to keep it going. Earnings Before Interest and Taxes (EBITDA) is a common measure of cash flow from core operations. It has the advantage of scrubbing out financing and tax strategies which vary from company to company.

Banks are interested in whether a company has enough cash to cover interest expense and other debt obligations such as mortgage, loan, sinking fund and lease payments. The Times Interest Earned and Debt Service Coverage ratios measure these items.

Burn rate is the monthly rate at which operations consume more cash than they generate. It can be used to forecast when a company will run out of money.

Tax strategy is also impacts cash flow. Tax accounting rules and GAAP accounting rules differ so most companies have two sets of books. Careful application of the tax code can allow a company to legally defer payment of some taxes. The time value of money means that if taxes can be deferred, a company can pay its tax obligation with cheaper future dollars.

CHAPTER 4

Asset Management

Introduction

Assets are all the "things" a company has to produce income. Examples of assets include cash, accounts and notes receivable, inventory, plant property and equipment, patents, copyrights, and goodwill. Assets must be financed, and they can only be financed with debt, money owed to others, or equity, the owner's investment in the company.

If a company has excess assets and they are financed by debt, a company will pay more interest than it has to. If a company has excess assets financed by owner's equity that means there is less money available for dividends or to finance expansion. So the first question that should be asked is whether a company has excess assets.

Assets

Return on Assets

Return on assets (ROA) indicates how effectively assets are being used to generate income. Some companies use minimal debt others use a lot of debt. To make companies comparable to one another, the effect of interest payments must be "scrubbed out." To do this add the after tax cost of net interest to net income. Net interest is interest expense less interest income. Multiplying net interest times one minus the tax rate gives the after tax cost of interest. Divide net income plus tax adjusted net interest by average assets to get ROA as shown in equation (4.1).

$$\text{ROA} = \frac{\text{Net Income} + \text{Interest (net)} \times (1 - \text{Tax Rate})}{(\text{Assets}_2 + \text{Assets}_1)/2} \quad (4.1)$$

Where Assets_2 and Assets_1 are total assets at the end of this year and last year respectively.

Suppose a company has net income of $12 million, interest expense of $4 million, interest income of $1 million, assets this year and last of $84 million and $80 million respectively and its effective tax rate is 33.33%. What is its ROA?

$$= \frac{\$12 \text{ million} + (\$4 \text{ million} - \$1 \text{ million}) \times (1 - 33.33\%)}{(\$84 \text{ million} + \$80 \text{ million}) / 2}$$

$$= \frac{\$12 \text{ million} + \$3 \text{ million} \times 66.67\%}{\$82 \text{ million}}$$

$$= \$14 \text{ million} / \$82 \text{ million}$$

$$= 17.1\%$$

Return on Assets is always stated as a percentage. If a company's ROA is low compared to its best competitors, that might indicate either (i) the company has too many assets, or (ii) management is not fully utilizing the assets it has. If the company has too many assets they should be identified and sold to raise cash.

A limitation to this ratio is that it has no meaning if adjusted net income is close to zero or negative.

Target Assets – Return on Assets Method

It's one thing to measure the efficiency of asset deployment, it's another to estimate how many assets a company should have. If a company has excess assets it must finance those assets with debt, which involves payment of interest, or equity which locks up capital that could be distributed to owners or used more productively to develop new products or expand in new markets.

The assets a company should have can be estimated by comparing the Return on Assets of a company's best competitors to the amount of adjusted income a company generates. Adjusted income is net income plus interest net of taxes. Equation (4.1) can be re-written as equation (4.2).

$$\text{ROA} = \frac{\text{Adjusted Net Income}}{\text{Average Assets}} \qquad (4.2)$$

Call the average ROA of a company's best competitors the Industry Average ROA and substitute Industry Average ROA for ROA in equation (4.2). Replace Average Assets with Target Assets, that is the estimate of the amount of assets a company should have given the income it is generating. With these substitutions and a little algebra, (4.2) can be re-written as equation (4.3).

$$\text{Target Assets} = \frac{\text{Adjusted Net Income}}{\text{Industry Average ROA}} \qquad (4.3)$$

Suppose a company has average assets of $12 million; Adjusted Net Income of $1.0 million and the Industry Average ROA is 11%. Estimate how much assets it should have.

$$= \frac{\$1,000,000}{11\%}$$

$$= \$9,090,909$$

The amount of excess assets is given by equation (4.4). Excess assets should be identified and sold to raise cash to pay down debt, distributed to owners, or invested in new products and markets.

Excess Assets= Average Assets – Target Assets   (4.4)

$$= \$12,000,000 - \$9,090,909$$

$$= \$2,909,091$$

This method cannot be used if a company's net income is negative or close to zero. None of the company's used to estimate the Industry Average ROA can have an a net income that is negative or close to zero.

Asset Turnover

Asset turnover is a measure of the efficiency with which assets are used to generate sales. The formula for Asset Turnover is given by equation (4.5).

$$\text{Asset Turnover} = \frac{\text{Sales}}{(\text{Assets}_2 + \text{Assets}_1) / 2} \qquad (4.5)$$

Where Assets_2 and Assets_1 are this year's and last year's total assets, respectively. Suppose a company has sales of $90 million and assets of $84 million and $80 million this year and last. What is its Asset Turnover?

$$= \frac{\$90 \text{ million}}{(\$84 \text{ million} + \$80 \text{ million}) / 2}$$

$$= \$90 \text{ million} / \$82 \text{ million}$$

$$= 1.1$$

Asset Turnover is a dimensionless number. The higher the Asset Turnover, the more efficient a company is at generating sales with the assets it has.

Target Assets – Asset Turnover Method

Asset Turnover proves a way to estimate a company's target assets and has the advantage that a company need not be profitable to use this method. In equation (4.5) replace Asset Turnover with Industry Average Asset Turnover and replace Average Assets with Target Assets which gives equation (4.6). With a little algebra, this can be converted to equation (4.7)

$$\text{Industry Average Asset Turnover} = \frac{\text{Sales}}{\text{Target Assets}} \qquad (4.6)$$

$$\text{Target Assets} = \frac{\text{Sales}}{\text{Industry Average Asset Turnover}} \qquad (4.7)$$

Suppose a company has Sales of $10.5 million, Assets of $12 million and the Industry Average Asset Turnover is 1.1. Estimate Target Assets.

$$= \frac{\$10,500,000}{1.1}$$

$$= \$9,545,455$$

There is no reason that target assets estimated using the ROA Method and target assets using the Asset Turnover Method should be exactly the same. Both are estimates. Estimates using two different methods are always better than an estimate using a single method. In theses examples, both estimates indicate the subject company has far more assets than needed considering its sales and adjusted net income.

Accounts Receivable

Accounts receivable is a listing of all money owed to the company by customers for credit sales.

Accounts Receivable Turnover

Accounts receivable turnover is a measure of the efficiency of the credit and collections department. The less efficient it is, the more cash is going to be tied up in accounts receivable. The more efficient it is, the more cash it will squeeze out of accounts receivable. The formula for Accounts Receivable (AR) Turnover is given by equation (4.8).

$$\text{AR Turnover} = \frac{\text{Net Credit Sales}}{(AR_2 + AR_1)/2} \qquad (4.8)$$

Where net credit sales are sales on credit less returns and allowances; AR_2 and AR_1 are the accounts receivable balances for this year and last respectively.

Most companies either sell for cash, or they sell on credit. Retailers sell for cash. Sales paid by cash, check, debit card, or credit card are all cash sales from the company's point of view. This ratio has no meaning for a company with all cash sales. Most business to business sales are on credit. In rare circumstances, a company will have both cash and credit sales. In those circumstances there must be some means of distinguishing between cash and credit sales before this ratio can be applied.

Suppose a company has net credit sales of $90 million and accounts receivable balances of $11 million and $9 million this year and last. What is its AR Turnover?

$$= \frac{\$90 \text{ million}}{(\$11 \text{ million} + \$9 \text{ million})/2}$$

$$= \$90 \text{ million} / \$10 \text{ million}$$

$$= 9.0$$

AR Turnover is a dimensionless number. The higher the AR Turnover the better.

Days Sales Outstanding (DSO)

AR Turnover is difficult for people without accounting training to conceptualize. A more intuitive measure of the efficiency of credit and collections is Days Sales Outstanding (DSO) which is an estimate of the average number of days it takes to collect credit sales. The formula for DSO is given by equation (4.9).

DSO= 365 days / AR Turnover   (4.9)

Suppose a company has an AR Turnover of 9.0. How many days does it take to collect its credit sales on average?

$$= 365 / 9.0$$

$$= 40.6 \text{ days}$$

DSO is quoted in number of days.

Accounts Receivable Performance Targets

Accounts Receivable (AR) represent loans to customers and as such it ties up capital which must be financed with either debt or equity. Aggressive accounts receivable management can squeeze cash out of accounts receivable. Setting credit and collection goals is as important as measuring credit and collection efficiency.

One way to set collection performance targets is to start with the amount of cash one wants to squeeze out of accounts receivable and see how that translates into performance targets. To squeeze cash out of accounts receivables means average accounts receivable must be reduced by some amount. This will give rise to a New AR Turnover as shown in equation (4.10).

$$\text{New AR Turnover} = \frac{\text{Credit Sales}}{\text{Average AR} - \text{Amount Raised}} \qquad (4.10)$$

Suppose a company had $90.0 million in sales, Average AR of $12.6 million and it wanted to raise $2.0 million in cash. The current AR Turnover is 7.14 ($90.0 million / $12.6 million). What would their New AR Turnover have to be to raise $2.0 million from accounts receivable?

$$= \frac{\$90.0M}{(\$12.6.0M - \$2.0M)}$$

$$= 8.49$$

Using equation (4.9) we can translate current performance and goal performance into DSO (average collection time). Currently DSO is 51.1 days (365 days / 7.14). If new performance targets are met, DSO should drop to 43.0 days (365 days / 8.49).

Sometimes a company finds its credit and collections efforts are less efficient than either industry norms, or its best competitors. The issue then is how much cash can be squeezed out of accounts receivable if the average number of days it takes to collect (DSO) are reduced to the selected target performance. Equation (4.9) gives the relationship between DSO and AR Turns. Substituting Target DSO for DSO and substituting New AR Turns for AR Turns and using algebra, equation (4.9) can be transformed into equation (4.11).

$$\text{New AR Turns} = 356 / \text{Target DSO} \qquad (4.11)$$

Equation (4.8) gives the relationship between AR Turns and Average AR. Substituting New AR Turns for AR Turns and New Average AR for Average AR and using a little algebra gives equation (4.12).

$$\text{New Average AR} = \frac{\text{Credit Sales}}{\text{New AR Turns}} \qquad (4.12)$$

Suppose a company has credit sales of $90.0 million, average accounts receivable of $12.6 million, the average DSO for the company's three best competitors is 40 days, and the company's goal is to beat this average by 10%. Its Target DSO is then 36 days (40 days – 10% x 40 days). Using equation (4.11) we can find its New AR Turnover.

New AR Turnover   = 365 / 36 days

                    = 10.14

With the New AR Turnover and equation (4.12) we can find the New Average AR.

New Average AR   = $90.0 million / 10.14

                = $8.9 million

Setting and achieving the target DSO in this example will squeeze $3.7 million of cash ($12.6million - $8.9 million) from the company's accounts receivable.

Inventory

Inventory is a class of assets purchased or manufactured for sale. For a manufacturing company, there are three classes of inventory: raw materials, work-in-process, and finished goods. Work-in-process inventory is raw materials to which some labor has been applied, but it is not quite finished.

Inventory Turnover

For a retailer, a high inventory turnover means it is selecting goods that customers want and that sell quickly. A low retail inventory turnover may mean less desirable goods are being purchased or that too many goods are being purchased.

In a manufacturing company, a low inventory turnover may mean too much raw material is being purchased, too many finished goods are being produced, or the manufacturing processes are inefficient causing delays on the factory floor. The formula for Inventory Turnover is given by equation (4.13).

$$\text{Inventory Turns} = \frac{\text{Cost of Goods Sold}}{(\text{Inventory}_2 + \text{Inventory}_1) / 2} \qquad (4.13)$$

Where Inventory_2 and Inventory_1 are total inventory this year and last. Suppose a company had cost of goods sold of $60 million, and inventory this year and last was $9 million and $7 million. What is inventory turnover?

$$= \frac{\$60 \text{ million}}{(\$9 \text{ million} + \$7 \text{ million}) / 2}$$

$$= \ \$60 \text{ million} / \$8 \text{ million}$$

$$= \ 7.5$$

Inventory turnover is always a dimensionless number. The higher the inventory turnover, the better.

Days In Inventory (DII)

Inventory turnover is a somewhat abstract measure of inventory management efficiency which makes it hard for non-accountants to understand. A more intuitive measure is Days in Inventory (DII). This estimates the average number of days a retailer takes to sell its goods. For a manufacturer, DII is the interval between the acquisition of raw materials and the disposition of finished goods. The formula for DII is given by equation (4.14).

$$\text{DII} = 365 \text{ days / Inventory Turnover} \qquad (4.14)$$

Suppose a company has an inventory turnover of 7.5. What is its DII?

$$= 365 \text{ days / 7.5}$$

$$= 48.7 \text{ days}$$

DII is always quoted in days. If a retailer's DII is greater than its competitors that may mean that it is purchasing goods customers don't want or it may mean the retailer's prices are too high. If a manufacturer's DII is greater than that of its competitors, it may mean it is purchasing too much raw materials, it is producing more than can be sold in a timely manner, it has obsolete or damaged inventory or that its production is inefficient.

Inventory Performance Targets

Setting and achieving inventory management targets can squeeze cash out of inventory. Careful inventory management can also reduce costs from obsolescence, storage, insurance and taxes.

One way to think about this is to ask what performance standard would have to be met to squeeze a certain amount of cash out of inventory. Squeezing cash out of inventory means reducing the average amount invested in inventory. The amount to be raised from inventory is equal to the amount by which average inventory must shrink. Substitute New Inventory Turns for Inventory Turnover in equation (4.13) which can be modified to provide equation (4.15) the performance target needed to raise a certain amount of cash from inventory.

$$\text{New Inventory Turns} = \frac{\text{COGS}}{\text{Average Inventory } - \text{ Amount Raised}} \qquad (4.15)$$

Suppose a company has COGS of $60.0 million, average inventory of $8.0 million and wishes to raise $1.0 million from inventory. What will their New Inventory Turns need to be?

$$= \frac{\$60.0 \text{ million}}{\$8 \text{ million} - \$1.0 \text{ million}}$$

$$= \$60.0 \text{ million} / \$7.0 \text{ million}$$

$$= 8.57$$

Using equation (4.14) this performance target can be translated into 42.6 day in inventory. Increasing throughput by just 6.1 days will reduce average inventory by $1.0 million.

Another way to think about stetting performance standards is to consider industry norms. Suppose a company's best competitors turnover inventory in 46 days and the company's goal is to beat its best competitors by 10%. That means they have to turnover inventory in an average of 41.4 days (46 days – 10% x 46 days). How much cash can be generated from meeting this performance target?

Equation (4.14) provides the relationship between Days in Inventory (DII) and Inventory Turnover. Substituting Target DII for DII and New Inventory Turns for Inventory Turnover and using a little algebra, this relationship can be re-written as equation (4.16).

New Inventory Turns= 365 / Target DII   (4.16)

Equation (4.13) provides the relationship between Cost of Goods Sold (COGS) and Average Inventory. Substituting New Inventory Turns for Inventory Turns, and New Average Inventory for Average Inventory, and with a little algebra, equation (4.13) can be re-written as equation (4.17).

New Average Inventory= COGS / New Inventory Turns   (4.17)

Suppose a company has a Target DII of 41.4 days, COGS of $60.0 million, and current average inventory of $8.0 million. Using equation (4.16),

New Inventory Turns= 365 days / 41.4 days

= 8.82

Using equation (4.17) gives New Average Inventory.

New Average Inventory= $60.0 million / 8.82

= $6.8 million

Achieving the new Target DII will reduce inventory by $1.2 million ($8.0 million old average inventory - $6.8 million New Average Inventory).

Identifying Excess Inventory

Inventory Turnover and DII provide a high level picture of whether inventory is being effectively managed. In most companies, some items move in and out of inventory rapidly, and some stays in inventory for very long periods of time. Think of this as an example of the 80-20 Rule. Eighty percent of sales probably come from twenty percent of the inventory items.

Virtually all inventory systems are computerized and items are identified by a part number or Stock Keeping Unit (SKU) number. Slow moving inventory and items that are overstocked can be identified for liquidation by computing the DII on a product by product basis. Use equation (4.13) for product level Inventory Turns and equation (4.14) for product level DII. Combining the two equations gives equation (4.18). This equation requires a rolling 12 month product level COGS. This is a fairly simple matter for computerized systems. Historical information on cost and sales must be captured at a product level to properly price inventory for FIFO and other cost systems.

$$\text{Product Level DII} = \frac{365 \text{ days x Product Inventory}}{\text{Rolling 12 Month COGS}} \qquad (4.18)$$

By using a rolling 12 month COGS a company can continuously monitor for excess inventory not just find excess inventory at year end. Using a rolling 12 month COGS automatically adjusts DII for chances in demand.

Suppose a company has two products, 1" diameter steel bars that cost $30 each, and 2" diameter steel bars that cost $70 each. It has $40,000 of 1" diameter steel bars in inventory and in the last 12 months it has sold 1" steel bars costing $700,000. It has $25,000 of 2" steel bars in inventory and in the last 12 months it has sold 2" steel bars with a cost of $90,000. What is the DII for each product?

$$\text{DII 1" bars} = \frac{365 \text{ days x } \$40,000}{\$700,000}$$

$$= 20.9 \text{ days}$$

$$\text{DII 2" bars} = \frac{365 \text{ days x } \$25,000}{\$90,000}$$

$$= 101.4 \text{ days}$$

If the company sets a standard of having not more than a 30 day supply of inventory on hand, it is managing its 1" bar stock very well. However, it has excess 2" stock.

Average Daily Sales Units

From the information needed to identify slow moving inventory, average inventory usage can be computed using equation (4.19).

$$\text{Average Daily Utilization} = \frac{\text{Rolling 12 month COGS}}{365 \text{ days x Cost per Unit}} \quad (4.19)$$

Suppose 1" steel bars cost $30 each and 2" steel bars cost $70 each. Using this and data from the example above, daily utilization can be estimated.

$$\text{Average Daily Utilization 1"} = \frac{\$700,000}{365 \text{ days x } \$30}$$
$$= 63.9 \text{ units / day}$$

$$\text{Average Daily Utilization 2"} = \frac{\$90,000}{365 \text{ days x } \$70}$$
$$= 3.5 \text{ units / day}$$

If the target inventory is a 30 days supply, the company should only have 105 units of 2" steel bars in stock (30 days x 3.5 units / day) at a value of $7,350. The facts in this problem indicate it has $25,000 of 2" steel bars in stock for excess inventory of about $17,650.

Once management sets the number of days of stock required for each item of inventory, computer reports can be set up fairly easily to identify excess inventory so it can be sold to raise cash.

Plant, Property & Equipment

Plant Turnover

Plant Turnover is a measure of the efficiency of plant in generating sales. On most Balance Sheets, Plant, Property and Equipment (PP&E) is recorded together, net of accumulated depreciation. PP&E includes assets to make products as well as assets used for overhead such as office buildings, furniture and computers. Plant Turnover can be computed using equation (4.20).

$$\text{Plant Turnover} = \text{Sales / PP\&E} \quad (4.20)$$

Suppose a company has sales of $90.0 million and PPE of $50.0 million. What is its Plant Turnover?

$$= \$90.0 / \$50.0$$
$$= 1.8$$

Plant Turnover is a dimensionless number. The higher the Plant Turnover the better. Plant Turnover represents the number of dollars of sales that each dollar of PP&E generates. If Plant Turnover is significantly lower than a company's best competitors, it may mean a company has too much PP&E or that it is purchasing buildings, equipment, furniture, cars, trucks and computers that are more expensive than needed.

Some caution that two companies may have a different Plant Turnover because one company has all new PP&E whereas the other company is using fully depreciated PP&E. This is a valid consideration, but should not be used as excuse. Purchase of fully functional used equipment is one way to improve Plant Turnover, as is purchase of less expensive facilities, furniture and fixtures. In addition, a poor Plant Turnover ratio may indicate a company has too many unproductive or under-producing assets

Performance Standards for PP&E

Equation (4.18) can be modified to set Plant Turnover goals by substituting Industry Average Plant Turnover for Plant Turnover, Target PP&E for PP&E and using algebra to get equation (4.21).

Target PP&E= Sales / Industry Average Plant Turnover   (4.21)

Suppose a company has $90 million in sales, and the Industry Average PP&E is 2.0. What should the company's Target PP&E be?

= $90.0 million / 2.0

= $45.0 million

This means the company has $5.0 million more PP&E than it needs to generate sales ($50.0 million current PP&E - $45.0 million Target PP&E). Look for excess PP&E in the company's fixed asset register. This is a list of assets the accounting department must maintain to compute depreciation. Excess assets should be identified and sold off to raise cash.

Imputed Interest

Interest on debt drags down net income. Selling off excess assets creates an opportunity to reduce debt and reduce interest expense. Calculating imputed interest provides a means for estimating the income statement impact of reducing a company's debt.

Imputed interest is net financing costs, usually interest expense less interest income divided by interest bearing liabilities as shown in equation (4.23).

$$\frac{\text{Imputed Interest}}{\text{Rate}} = \frac{\text{Interest Exp. + Other Financing Costs} - \text{Interest Income}}{\text{Interest Bearing Liabilities}} \quad (4.24)$$

Imputed interest is a rough estimate of the cost of financing interest bearing liabilities. Interest is not paid on all liabilities. For example, interest is not paid on accounts payable, accrued payroll or deferred taxes. So reducing these liabilities will not reduce interest expense. However, interest is paid on a line of credit, bank term loans, bonds, mortgages, credit card interest and capital leases. Other financing costs include credit card discounts, if the company accepts credit cards, as well as discounts on notes, commercial paper and factored accounts receivable.

Suppose a company pays $80,000 interest on bank loans; $200,000 on bonds; expenses $40,000 on note discounts; it earns $20,000 per year on interest; bank loans total $900,000 and bonds total $3,100,000. What is its imputed interest rate?

$$\text{Imputed Interest Rate} = \frac{\$80,000 + \$200,000 + \$40,000 - \$20,000}{\$900,000 + \$3,100,000}$$

$$= \$300,000 / \$4,000,000$$

$$= 7.5\%$$

Identifying excess assets; converting them to cash; and paying down debt will reduce the amount of interest paid. Reducing interest payments increases both net income and cash flow. The increase in net income is given by equation (4.25).

Increase in Net Income = Imputed Interest Rate   (4.25)

x Net Interest Bearing Debt Paid Down

x (1- Tax Rate)

Suppose a company has $4,000,000 of interest bearing debt at an imputed interest rate of 7.5% and the company's tax rate is 30%. Using techniques discussed earlier in the chapter, the company identifies $700,000 of excess assets which it converts to cash. Estimate the increase in net income from using the cash raised to pay down debt.

Increase in Net Income = 7.5% x $700,000 x (1 – 30%) = $36,750

The rational for the tax adjustment is that net income is an after tax measure.

Conclusion

Assets are all the things a company owns. Assets are financed with either debt or equity. Excess assets mean a company will have an unnecessary debt burden or it will tie up owners' equity.

Return on Assets and Asset Turnover can be used to measure the efficiency with which management is using assets and, when compared to industry norms, can be used to set target levels of assets. The difference between target levels of assets and actual assets represents excess assets that should be identified and sold to raise cash.

Accounts receivable is a list of customers that owe the company money. The efficiency of the credit and collections department can be determined through the Accounts Receivable Turnover ratio and the Days Sales Outstanding ratio. These ratios can be combined with industry norms to set credit and collections performance standards. A company can also base performance targets on how much cash it plans to squeeze out of accounts receivable.

Inventory is goods held for sale in the ordinary course of business plus raw materials and partially completed goods. Partially completed goods are called Work In Process inventory. The Inventory Turnover and Days in Inventory ratios can be used to measure the efficiency of management. Combined with industry norms, these ratios can be used to set performance standards. Inventory Turnover and Days in Inventory can be applied to individual items of inventory to identify slow moving items which should be sold wholesale to raise cash.

Plant Turnover is a measure of the efficiency of plant, property and equipment (PP&E) in generating sales. Combined with industry norms, it can estimate the amount of PP&E a company should have so that any excess can be identified and sold to raise cash.

Asset management is a critical element in driving a company to superior performance because improper management will lead to investing capital in unproductive assets. Capital invested, or locked up in unproductive assets cannot be used to grow a company.

CHAPTER 5

Credit-worthiness

Introduction

It's not just banks that should be concerned with a company's creditworthiness. Suppliers that sell to a company on credit and those who buy a company's bonds should also be concerned with whether it can pay its bills. Customers should be concerned because they don't want to buy a product that needs servicing from a company about to go out of business and employees want to know that a company can meet its payroll.

Current Ratio

The current ratio is a measure of whether a company can pay its bills with current assets. The current ratio is current assets divided by current liabilities. Current assets include cash and assets expected to be converted to cash within a year. Examples of current assets include accounts receivable, inventory and notes receivable expected to be collected within a year. Current liabilities are debts that must be paid within a year. Examples of current liabilities include accounts payable, accrued payroll, a line of credit, notes payable within a year and bank loan principal due within a year. The formula for current ratio is given by equation (5.1).

$$\text{Current Ratio} = \frac{\text{Current Assets}}{\text{Current Liabilities}} \tag{5.1}$$

Suppose a company has cash of $8 million, accounts receivable of $28 million, inventory of $32 million, accounts payable of $16 million, accrued payroll of $1 million, and principal payments on a bank loan due within a year of $5 million. What is its current ratio?

$$= \frac{\$8 \text{ million} + \$28 \text{ million} + \$32 \text{ million}}{\$16 \text{ million} + \$1 \text{ million} + \$5 \text{ million}}$$

= $68 million / $22 million

= 3.09

The current ratio is a dimensionless number. A current ratio of 1.0 or less is always bad. How high the current ratio should be is determined by industry averages. Banks like the current ratio to be in the upper 25% of industry averages.

Quick Ratio

The Quick Ratio, also called the Acid Test Ratio, is current assets less inventory divided by current liabilities. Banks don't understand inventory so they want to know whether other current assets are sufficient to pay current liabilities. The formula for the Quick Ratio is given by equation (5.2).

$$\text{Quick Ratio} = \frac{\text{Current Assets} - \text{Inventory}}{\text{Current Liabilities}} \qquad (5.2)$$

Suppose a company has cash of $8 million, accounts receivable of $28 million, inventory of $32 million, accounts payable of $16 million, accrued payroll of $1 million, and principal payments on a bank loan of $5 million. What is its Quick Ratio?

$$= \frac{\$8 \text{ million} + \$28 \text{ million}}{\$16 \text{ million} + \$1 \text{ million} + \$5 \text{ million}}$$

= $36 million / $22 million

= 1.64

The Quick Ratio is a dimensionless number. Banks like the Quick Ratio to be in the upper 25% of industry averages.

Debt Equity Ratio

The debt equity ratio is shown in equation (5.3). It is a measure of the relative risk of those lending money to a company. Since debtors get paid before those with an equity position, equity represents a kind of buffer or shield protecting creditors. The more equity, the more protection for creditors. Total liabilities from the Balance Sheet is used for Debt in this equation.

Debt Equity Ratio= Debt / Equity   (5.3)

Suppose a company has Assets of $600, Liabilities of $400 and Equity of $200. What is its Debt Equity Ratio?

= $400 / $200

= 2.0

The lower the Debt Equity Ratio, the greater the cushion creditors have if the company runs into trouble.

Debt Ratio

The Debt Ratio, shown in equation (5.4) represents the percentage of assets financed by creditors. If the Debt Ratio gets too high, there is little cushion for creditors if the company gets into trouble.

Debt Ratio= Debt / Assets (5.4)

Suppose a company has $600 in assets and $400 in liabilities. What is its Debt Ratio?

= $400 / $600

= 66.7%

The issue for banks and other creditors is whether there will be enough value in assets to pay outstanding debts. Many times assets sell for less than book value. In addition, brokers are generally needed to sell assets and their commissions further reduce the amount available to cover debts. If a company's debt ratio rises above 80%, there is a substantial question as to whether assets will be sufficient to pay creditors.

Customer Concentration

If a company's sales are concentrated in a few customers, loss of one or two customers can jeopardize its solvency. When a company goes public, it often discloses the percent of sales to its top ten customers to warn investors of this risk. Concentration is sales to a particular customer divided by total sales as shown in equation (5.5).

Customer Concentration$_i$= Sales$_i$ / Sales (5.5)

Where Customer Concentration$_i$ is percentage of sales to the ith customer, Sales$_i$ is the sales in dollars to the ith customer and Sales is total company sales.

Suppose a company has twenty customers and the sales to these customers ranked from the greatest to least are $80, $50, $30, $20 and sales to the remaining sixteen customers total $20. Sales to all customers is $200. What is the concentration ratio for each of the top four customers?

Customer1= $80 / $200= 40%

Customer2= $50 / $200= 25%

Customer3= $30 / $200= 15%

Customer4= $20 / $200= 10%

Loss of either of the top two customers could be fatal to the company because the company is so dependent on those sales. Loss of customers three and four could jeopardize profits and cash flow. Loss of one of the sixteen smaller customers would simply be an inconvenience. Where no customer represents more than one percent of sales, this ratio has little meaning.

Accounts Receivable Aging

The older an account receivable is, the less likely it is to be collected. If a customer is willing an able to pay, it would do so sooner rather than later. Banks do not consider accounts receivable (AR) older than 90 days an asset, some do not consider AR over 60 days old an asset and most public accounting firms require AR over 180 days old to be written off or fully reserved in the Allowance for Doubtful Accounts.

Accounts receivable are usually classified into brackets which measure how long the invoice has been outstanding. These brackets are 0-30 days, 31-60 days, 61 to 90 days, 91 to 180 days, and over 180 days. A large percentage of AR should be in the 0-30 day bracket, with some percentage in the 31-60 day bracket. Except when billing the Federal Government, anything over 60 days is trouble.

Accounts receivable aging for each bracket can be expressed as a ratio of the dollars in that bracket to total accounts receivable as shown in equation (5.6). Expressing AR Aging as bracket percent provides a better perspective on credit and collections than simply reporting dollars by brackets.

Bracket% = Bracket AR / Total AR $\qquad$ (5.6)

Suppose a company has 300 of AR, of which 190 was 0-30 days old, 60 was 31 to 60 days old, 30 was 61 to 90 days old, 15 was 91 to 180 days old and 5 was over 180 days old.

$$
\begin{aligned}
\text{AR00-30} &= 190/300 = 63.3\% \\
\text{AR31-60} &= 60/300 = 20.0\% \\
\text{AR61-90} &= 30/300 = 10.0\% \\
\text{AR91-180} &= 15/300 = 5.0\% \\
\text{AR Over 180} &= 5/300 = 1.7\%
\end{aligned}
$$

A company with more than 5% of its accounts receivable over 60 days old is doing something wrong. Either is not doing a good job of credit underwriting (selecting who it will extend credit to) or it is selling goods or services that are so defective customers are refusing to pay.

Doubtful Accounts Ratio

Accounts receivable are reported as an asset on the balance sheet net of an Allowance for Doubtful Accounts. The allowance for doubtful accounts is an estimate of the amount of AR that can probably never be collected. The ratio of the Allowance for Doubtful Accounts to AR gives an indication of the efficiency of credit and collections.

Typically companies report Accounts Receivable (AR) net of Allowance for Doubtful Accounts. To get Total Accounts Receivable one must add Accounts Receivable Net to the Allowance. The Doubtful Accounts (DA) ratio is given by equation (5.7).

$$\frac{\text{Doubtful Accounts}}{\text{Ratio}} = \frac{\text{Allowance for Doubtful Accounts}}{\text{AR Net of Allowance} + \text{Allowance for Doubtful Accounts}} \quad (5.7)$$

Suppose a company reports Accounts Receivable of $1,000 net of an allowance for doubtful accounts of $90. What is the Doubtful Accounts Ratio?

$$= \frac{\$90}{1,000 + 90}$$

$$= \$90 / \$1090$$

$$= 8.3\%$$

A company with a Doubtful Accounts ratio over about 3% is not effectively underwriting (evaluating) customer credit worthiness or it is selling goods and services that are so poor customers are refusing to pay. Ideally, a Doubtful Accounts ratio should be less than 1%. It is impossible for this ratio to be zero.

Days To Pay

One way to improve Days Sales Outstanding (DSO) and Accounts Receivable Turnover is through credit analysis. If a customer pays other suppliers slowly, it is likely to pay your company slowly. Days to Pay (DTP) is the average number of days it takes a customer to pay its bills as shown in equation (5.8).

$$\text{Days To Pay} = 365 \text{ days} / \text{AP Turnover} \quad (5.8)$$

Accounts payable turnover is given by equation (5.9).

$$\text{AP Turnover} = \frac{\text{Purchases}}{(AP_2 + AP_1)/2} \quad (5.9)$$

Where AP_2 is the customer's current year end accounts payable, AP_1 is the customer's prior year accounts payable. Accounts payable can be found on the customer's Balance Sheet. While Purchases is not reported on any financial statement, it can be computed from information that is reported as shown in equation (5.10).

Purchases= COGS + Ending Inventory – Beginning Inventory   (5.10)

Cost of Goods Sold, as well as beginning and ending inventory can be found on the Income Statement and Balance Sheet respectively. If a company is publicly traded, its financial statements can be found on the Securities and Exchange Commission website www.sec.gov. If it is not publicly traded, and it is asking for a substantial amount of credit (more than one day's net income) it should fill out a credit application and attach its financial statements. If it is privately held and refuses to provide financial statements, it should provide the five variables needed to compute days to pay (i) Accounts Payable at the end of the most current and (ii) prior year, (iii) COGS, (iv) Beginning Inventory and (v) Ending Inventory. The credit application should also ask whether the company is profitable, solvent and not contemplating bankruptcy. If the customer refuses to provide even this minimal level of information, the company should not extend it credit. It should only sell to the customer for cash in advance.

Suppose a customer has COGS of $50.0 million, Beginning Inventory of $10.0 million, Ending Inventory of $12.0 million, AP_2 and AP_1 of $7.0 and $6.0 million respectively.

Purchases= $50.0 million + $12.0 million - $10.0 million

= $52.0 million

$$AP\ Turnover= \frac{\$52.0\ million}{(\$7.0\ million + \$6.0\ million)/2}$$

= 8.0

DTP= 365 days / 8.0

= 45.6 days

If a company's goal is to reduce DSO to 36 days, it shouldn't sell on credit to a company which routinely pays its bills in 45.6 days. While this computation may seem complex, the formulae can be set up on a spreadsheet so that each equation feeds the next. Then, for each new customer the company need only input the five variables above.

Customer Payment Performance

Another way to reduce DSO is to constantly monitor old outstanding accounts receivables. Just as DSO can be computed for accounts receivable in the aggregate, DSO can be measured for individuals companies. Equation (4.8) and (4.9) are combined into equation (5.11). Average accounts receivable are replaced by the customer's accounts receivable balance. This ratio requires maintaining sales by customer on a rolling 12 month basis. This is a fairly simple matter for computerized systems.

$$\text{Customer DSO} = \frac{365 \text{ days x Outstanding Customer AR Balance}}{\text{Rolling 12 Month Sales to Customer}} \qquad (5.11)$$

Some ratios are too important to defer until the end of the year or even the end of a quarter. This report should be run at least weekly, and perhaps daily, sorted from the highest Customer DSO to the lowest Customer DSO. This analysis will keep slow pay customers clearly in focus. Those with a DSO greater than the target DSO should be singled out for special collection attention.

Suppose Alice Industries has an outstanding Accounts Receivable balance of $100,000 and the rolling twelve months sales to Alice Industries was $1,300,000. Bob Company has an Accounts Receivable balance of $50,000 and the rolling twelve month sales to Bob Company was $400,000. What is the Customer DSO of each?

$$\text{Alice Industries DSO} = \frac{365 \text{ days x } \$100,000}{\$1,300,000}$$

$$= 28.1 \text{ days}$$

$$\text{Bob Company DSO} = \frac{365 \text{ days x } \$50,000}{\$400,000}$$

$$= 45.6 \text{ days}$$

The distinction between Days to Pay and Customer DSO is that Days to Pay is designed to pre-screen new customers. Customer DSO is used to focus credit and collection attention on existing customers who need the most attention and ultimately decide when to cut off credit.

Z Score

A Z Score can be used by banks and investors to assess the financial health of a company. The Z Score is a weighted average of financial ratios as shown in equation (5.12).[1]

< 1.81	Company is unhealthy. Probability of failure is high
1.81 - 2.99	Gray area. Further investigation is required.
> 2.99	Company is healthy.

$X1 =$ Working Capital/Total Assets
$X2 =$ Retained Earnings/Total Assets
$X3 =$ Earnings Before Taxes & Interest / Total Assets

[1] The Z-Score was developed by Professor Edward Altman in the late 1960s and still considered to have predictive power. See Workouts and Turnarounds - The Handbook of Restructuring and Investing In Distressed Companies, DiNapoli, Sigoloff & Cushman, Editors, Business One Irwin, Homewood, Ill. p. 27.

X4 = Market Value of Equity / Total Liabilities
X5 = Sales / Total Assets

$$Z = 1.2* X1 + 1.4* X2 + 3.3* X3 + 6.0* X4 + 1.0* X5 \qquad (5.12)$$

Suppose companies A and B had the ratios listed below. Would they be healthy enough to extend credit to, buy the bonds of, or invest in?

	A Company	B Company
Working Capital/Total Assets (X1)	.20	.20
Retained Earnings/Total Assets (X2)	.30	.02
EBIT / Total Assets (X3)	.10	.00
Market Value / Total Liabilities (X4)	.35	.11
Sales / Total Assets (X5)	1.09	.09

Z Score A Company= $1.2 * .20 + 1.4 * .3 + 3.3* .10 + 6.0 * .35 + 1.0 * 1.09$

$= .24 + .42 + .33 + 2.1 + 1.09$

$= 4.18$

Z Score B Company= $1.2 * .20 + 1.4 * .02 + 3.3 * .00 + 6.0 * .11 + 1.0 * .09$

$= .24 + .03 + 0.0 + .66 + .09$

$= 1.02$

Whereas the Z-Score indicates Company A is healthy and in no danger of failing, Company B is unhealthy and the probability of failure is high.

Borrowing Capacity

While borrowing capacity is not, strictly speaking a ratio, it is an important determinant of how much a bank will lend to a given customer. A high borrowing capacity does not necessarily mean a bank will lend to a given company. Think of borrowing capacity as an upper limit on how much a bank will lend.

Borrowing capacity is tangible net worth times some factor. Tangible net worth is tangible assets less non-bank liabilities. Tangible assets excludes patents, copyrights, goodwill, pre-paid expenses (for most banks), loans to officers, directors and employees and accounts receivable over 90 days old (over 60 days old for some banks).

Suppose a company has $1,000 of assets, but listed among its assets are Copyrights $10, Patents $20, Goodwill $100, loans to officers, directors and employees of $20, pre-paid expenses of $10, and accounts receivable over 90 days of $40. Further suppose the company has Non-bank liabilities including accounts payable of $300, notes payable to trade vendors of $20, lease obligations not payable to the bank of $40. The factor the bank uses to discount Tangible net worth to get borrowing capacity is 80% (some banks use 70%). What is the company's borrowing capacity?

Assets	$1,000
less excluded items	
Copyrights	$10
Patents	20
Goodwill	100
Loans to officers, etc.	20
Pre-paid expenses	10
AR over 90 days	40
	200
Tangible Assets	$800
Less Non-bank Liabilities	
Accounts Payable	$300
Notes Payable Trade	20
Leases	40
	$360
Tangible Net Worth	$440
x Factor	80%
Borrowing Capacity	$352

Most banks have a loan covenant (a promise to the bank) that requires a company to submit a certified copy of its Borrowing Capacity analysis every month. A certified copy is one which the controller or CFO attests to in writing. If a company's borrowing capacity deteriorates, bank loan agreements give it the right to accelerate (call in) the loan balance. If at any time the amount loaned by the bank exceeds a company's borrowing capacity, the company must repay the excess as soon as it is discovered.

Conclusion

Banks, investors, suppliers, management and even employees have an interest in whether a company has good credit. Companies also need to assess the creditworthiness of their customers.

Creditworthiness can be measured with Current and Quick ratios which assess whether a company has enough current assets to pay current liabilities; Debt to Equity and Debt Ratios which assess aggregate debt level; Customer Concentration which assesses how vulnerable a company is to loss of one or a few customers; Accounts Receivable Aging and Doubtful Accounts ratio which assess the likelihood that customers will pay their bills; Days to Pay which assesses whether a company should extend credit to a new customer; Customer DSO which is used to focus attention on slow pay customers; Z-Scores which rate the likelihood that a company will fail, and Borrowing Capacity which is a measure of how much credit a bank will extend to a company.

No single method is right for every set of circumstances, but two or more techniques taken together provide a fairly good indication of a company's creditworthiness.

CHAPTER 6
Staffing Ratios

Introduction

For most companies, labor is a significant expense. Labor costs include wages, salaries, fringe benefits, FICA tax, Medicare tax, unemployment compensation tax, and workers compensation premiums. Employees also use space, heat, light, furniture, fixtures and equipment and telecommunications.

An important element of profitability is having the right number of people. If a company has too few people, it will forego business opportunities it might otherwise have, may be chronically backlogged and may have excess turnover as overworked people quit. On the other hand, too many employees represent an avoidable cost.

Revenue per Employee

One way to estimate whether a company has an appropriate number of employees is to look at the average revenue generated per employee. No one expects janitors to close million dollar deals, but everyone on the payroll supports closing those deals in some manner. For this analysis sales is used to mean revenue. The formula for Revenue per Employee (RPE) is given by equation (6.1).

RPE= Sales / Number of Employees　　　　　　　　　　　　　　(6.1)

Suppose a company has sales of $20 million and 110 employees. What would its RPE be?

= $20,000,000 / 110

= $181,818 per employee

RPE is always quoted as dollars per employee. When computing RPE always write out sales in dollars. For example write $20 million as $20,000,000. This will dramatically reduce errors. If a company's employees are generating less revenue than its competitors, that is a signal that the company is over-staffed. However, if a company's RPE is somewhat greater than that of its competitors, staffing levels may be appropriate.

EBITDA per Employee

There is a long distance between sales and profits. An alternative way to determine whether a company has an appropriate number of employees is to compute EBITDA per Employee (EPE). EBITDA is earnings before interest and taxes (EBIT) plus depreciation and amortization. EBTDA is a rough estimate of cash generated by operations. Earnings before interest and taxes (EBIT) is found on the Income Statement. Depreciation and Amortization are found on the Statement of Cash Flows. The formula for EPE is given in equation (6.2).

$$EPE = \frac{EBITDA}{\text{Number of Employees}} \qquad (6.2)$$

Suppose a company has EBIT of $2.2 million, depreciation of $0.6 million, amortization of $0.2 million and 110 employees. What is its EPE?

$$= \frac{\$2,200,000 + \$600,000 + \$200,000}{110}$$

$$= \$3,000,000 \: / \: 110$$

$$= \$27,273 \text{ per employee}$$

EPE is quoted as dollars per employee. When computing EPE always write out EBIT, depreciation and amortization in dollars. For example write $2.2 million as $2,200,000. This will dramatically reduce errors. If a company's employees are generating less EBITDA per person than its competitors, that is a signal that the company is over-staffed. However, if a company's EPE is greater than that of its competitors, staff levels may be appropriate.

Target number of employees – Revenue method

How many employees should a company have? One way to estimate the number of employees a company should have is to compare its Revenue per Employee (RPE) to the Industry Average RPE. In equation (6.1) substitute Industry Average RPE for RPE, and Target Number of Employees for the Number of Employees. Using algebra this modified equation can be written as equation (6.3).

Target Number of Employees= Sales / Industry Average RPE   (6.3)

Suppose a company has $20,000,000 in sales, 110 employees and the Industry Average RPE is $204,000. About how many employees should it have?

= $20,000,000 / $204,000

= 98

This analysis indicates the company is overstaffed by about 12 employees (110 actual employees – 98 target number of employees). If the Target Number of Employees and the actual number of employees differs by 2% or 3% overstaffing is probably not an issue. However, where the difference is more than 5% a company should consider a headcount reduction. In this example the company is overstaffed by 12.2% ((110 actual – 98 target) / 98 target) the company should consider headcount reductions.

Target number of employees EBITDA method

A Target Number of Employees can also be estimated by modifying the EBITDA per Employee ratio (6.2). Substitute the Target Number of Employees for Number of Employees; substitute Industry Average EPE for EPE; and using algebra, one gets equation (6.4)

$$\text{Target Number of Employees} = \frac{\text{EBITDA}}{\text{Industry Average EPE}} \qquad (6.4)$$

Suppose a company has 110 employees, EBITDA of $3,000,000 and the Industry Average EPE is $29,700. Estimate the Target Number of Employees.

= $3,000,000 / $29,700

= 101

Based on this estimate, the company is overstaffed by about 9 people or 9% ((110 actual employees – 101 target number of employees) / 101 target employees). There is no reason the target number of employees should be the same when estimated by the revenue method and the EBITDA method. However, having two estimates is always better than one. In this example, the company should probably have between 98 and 101 employees.

The EBITDA method of estimating the target number of employees will not work if a company has an EBITDA that is zero, negative or close to zero. Companies used to compute Industry Average EPE cannot have an EBITDA that is zero, negative or close to zero.

Salary leverage

Salary leverage is the amount of sales generated by every dollar of salary. This ratio is more sensitive to high executive compensation than Revenue per Employee. The equation for salary leverage is given by equation (6.5).

Salary Leverage= Sales / Total Salaries   (6.5)

A version of this equation uses total compensation rather than total salaries in the denominator. Since it is difficult to find salaries of competing companies, this ratio can usually only be applied to a company's own historical performance. If salary leverage is decreasing, that means executives and other employees are taking relatively more out of the company in compensation than they are contributing.

Suppose a company had sales of $90.0 million this year and $88.0 million last year and total compensation of $18.0 million this year and $17.0 million last year.

$$\text{Current Year Salary Leverage} = \frac{\$90.0 \text{ million}}{\$18.0 \text{ million}}$$

$$= 5.0$$

$$\text{Last Year Salary Leverage} = \frac{\$88.0 \text{ million}}{\$17.0 \text{ million}}$$

$$= 5.18$$

Deteriorating salary leverage means executive and employee salary expectations are unrealistic or it can mean that headcount is increasing out of proportion to sales. Both alternatives signal trouble. Use the Revenue per Employee and EBIDTA per Employee to determine whether the company has too many employees. Use salary surveys to determine whether employees are overcompensated.

Span of control

Span of control is the number of people each manager supervises. Suppose each manager supervises six people; an Assistant Vice President supervises six managers, and a Vice President supervises six Assistant Vice Presidents, the span of control is six.

Assume for the moment that the workers making, selling and accounting for the goods and services of the company are all needed. Mangers, Assistant Vice Presidents and Vice Presidents are the middle management. Middle management is expensive and doesn't make, sell or count the product, so the question is how many middle managers should a company have? Increasing the span of control reduces the number of middle managers. The Span of Control can be estimated using equation (6.6).

$$S = \frac{E}{(E - W)} \qquad \qquad (6.6)$$

Where E is the total number of employees and W is the number of workers (non-managers). The quantity (E −W) is just the number of managers. The number of managers can be substituted into (6.6) to get (6.7) an estimate of the span of control.

$$S = \frac{E}{M} \qquad \qquad (6.7)$$

Suppose a company has 500 employees and 80 managers. What is its span of control?

$$= 500 / 80$$

$$= 6.3$$

A company's span of control should be compared to industry norms which might be available through trade journals. A company can also compare itself to its historical span of control.

If staffing ratios indicate a company is overstaffed and its span of control is in the single digits, it might consider reducing the number of middle managers. Suppose middle management in this example were reduced by 10. Reducing the number of middle managers by 10 reduces the total number of employees from 500 to 490. What is the new estimate of the span of control?

$$= 490 / 70$$

$$= 7$$

Estimating number of managers – Various spans of control

The number of managers needed with various spans of control can be roughly estimated by rewriting equation (6.7) to get equation (6.8).

$$M = E / S \qquad \qquad (6.8)$$

Suppose a company with 500 employees wants to implement a span of control of 8, how many managers would it need?

$$= 500 / 8$$

$$= 63$$

This is only a rough approximation because as the span of control increases, fewer managers will be needed. When fewer managers are used, the total number of employees shrinks, which will further reduce the number of mangers needed.

Suppose a company started with 500 employees of which 80 were managers. If the company's plan is to increase the span of control to 8, only 63 managers would be needed for a reduction of 17 employees (80 – 63). Total employees would now be only 483 (500 – 17). Plugging the new number of employees and a span of control of 8 into equation (6.8) gives

$$= 483 / 8$$

$$= 61$$

Reducing employment by another two managers from 63 to 61 and re-estimating the number of managers needed still yields 60 and a fraction mangers. As a general rule round up fractional managers to the next whole manager.

Employee turnover

Employee turnover is often a hidden cost. Few employees are productive the day they are hired. On-the-job training has a cost, as does the lack of productivity until an employee is fully up to speed on company operations. Recruiting new employees is also expensive. Define turnover as the number of new hires divided by the average head count as shown in equation (6.9). Why new hires and why not terminations? The reason is that on-the-job training costs are embedded in the new employees not the ones that have left.

$$\text{Turnover} = \frac{\text{New Hires}}{(E_2 + E_1)/2} \qquad (6.9)$$

Where E_2 is the year end employment, and E_1 is employment at the beginning of the year. Suppose a company had 120 employees at year end, 110 employees at the beginning of the year and it hired 80 employees. What is the company's Turnover?

$$= \frac{80}{(120 + 110)/2}$$

$$= 80 / 115$$

$$= 70\%$$

Employee turnover rates above 200% are not uncommon in restaurants, retailing and telemarketing. If a company's turnover rate is over 30%, it should probably investigate what it can do to reduce turnover.

Staff to line ratio

Line employees, are those that make the product, sell the product, count the product or manage those who do. Everyone else is a staff. Examples of staff include those who work in public relations, market research, human resources, custodial, security, strategic planning, mergers and acquisitions, and research and development.

When a company has too many staff employees in relation to line employees it is on its way to collapsing of because of excess bureaucracy. The ratio of staff to line employees is given by equation (6.10).

Staff to Line Ratio= Staff Employees / Line Employees   (6.10)

Suppose a company has 90 staff employees and 410 line employees. What is its Staff to Line Ratio?

   = 90 / 410

   = 22.0%

There is no ideal Staff to Line Ratio. However, if this ratio is large, as in this example, or it is small, but growing, a company is headed for trouble.

Conclusion

Optimizing the number of employees is crucial for a company's profitability; too few employees and a company could miss opportunities; too many employees and it will incur avoidable expenses.

Revenue per Employee (RPE) and EBITDA per Employee (EPE) can be used to estimate whether a company has an appropriate number of employees. Salary Leverage can be used to determine whether compensation is becoming excessive. Span of control can help determine whether a company has too many middle managers. The Employee Turnover ratio helps identify whether a company has hidden employment costs. The Staff to Line Ratio can help determine whether the mix of line and staff employees is appropriate.

Ratios can be used to identify waste and help determine appropriate employment, management, and staff levels.

CHAPTER 7

Executive Compensation

Introduction

Shareholders elect a board of directors and the board of directors selects the CEO. The CEO and other corporate executives are supposed to manage the company in the best interest of the shareholders. The issue is whether corporate executives are primarily looking out for the shareholders or themselves. In management literature this is called the agency problem. Do agents (corporate executives) really work in the best interests of their principals (the shareholders)? Extraordinary executive compensation has become common even when companies under-perform. This chapter provides some means of measuring the reasonableness of executive compensation.

Revenue to Executive compensation

The objective of this ratio is to determine whether executive compensation is growing faster than revenue. By comparing the ratio of revenue to executive compensation year over year, a board of directors or outside investors can get a sense of whether executives are looking after shareholder interests or their own. Many companies compute executive compensation as a percentage of sales. This usually results in such a small percentage that boards, shareholders and investors ignore it. On the other hand, this ratio throws trends in executive compensation into bold relief.

For public companies, compensation for the CEO, CFO and the top three other most highly compensated company employees can be found in its 10-K or Proxy Statement posted on the SEC's website www.sec.gov. For this ratio executive compensation is the total compensation for these officers. The ratio Revenue to Executive Compensation can be calculated using equation (7.1).

Revenue to Executive Compensation = Revenue / Executive Compensation   (7.1)

Suppose a company has revenue of $20 million and the top five executives have compensation of $700,000. What is Revenue to Executive Compensation?

= $20,000,000 / $700,000

= 28.57

If this ratio is increasing year to year, it means executives are generating relatively more in sales for each dollar of compensation. However, if this ratio is declining, that means executives are taking relatively more than they are contributing in the form of increased sales.

EBITDA to Executive compensation

The purpose of this ratio is to help boards of directors, investors and analysts evaluate whether executive compensation is unreasonable. Many companies compute executive compensation as a percentage of EBITDA. This results in a percentage that is so small it is ignored. The ratio of EBITDA to executive compensation, when analyzed on a year over year basis throws executive compensation into bold relief. EBITDA is Earnings before Interest and Taxes from the Income Statement plus Depreciation and Amortization from the Statement of Cash Flows. EBITDA is a rough estimate of the amount of cash generated from operations. Executive compensation is the compensation of the CEO, CFO and the three other most highly compensated employees. The ratio EBITDA to Executive Compensation can be computed using equation (7.2).

EBITDA to Executive Compensation= EBIDA / Executive Compensation   (7.2)

Suppose a company has EBITDA of $4 million and executive compensation of $700,000, what is the ratio of EBITDA to Executive Compensation?

= $4,000,000 / $700,000

= 5.71

If the ratio of EBITDA to Executive Compensation is declining year over year that means the company's top executives are appropriating more of shareholder's wealth each year. In fact, as the company grows, this ratio should rise fairly rapidly year over year.

Net income to Executive compensation

The purpose of this ratio is to help boards of directors, investors and analysts evaluate whether executive compensation is reasonable in light of a company's ability to generate net income. Many companies compute executive compensation as a percentage of Net

Income. The result is a percentage that is so small it is ignored. The ratio of Net Income to executive compensation, when analyzed on a year over year basis provides a much clearer picture as to whether executive compensation is disproportionate to results. Executive compensation is the compensation of the CEO, CFO and the three other most highly compensated employees. The ratio Net Income to Executive Compensation can be computed using equation (7.3).

$$\text{Net Income to Executive Compensation} = \text{Net Income/Executive Compensation} \qquad (7.3)$$

Suppose a company has Net Income of $2 million and executive compensation of $700,000. What is the ratio of Net Income to Executive Compensation?

$$= \$2,000,000 / \$700,000$$

$$= 2.86$$

This ratio should increase year over year if executive management is doing its job effectively. A steady or declining Net Income to Executive Compensation ratio means management is not earning its compensation.

Growth in executive compensation

Growth in Executive Compensation is the year over year change in the compensation of the CEO, CFO and the other three highest compensated officers as shown in equation (7.4).

$$\text{Growth in Exec. Compensation} = \frac{\text{Exec. Comp.}_2 - \text{Exec. Comp.}_1}{\text{Exec. Comp.}_1} \qquad (7.4)$$

Where Exec. Comp.$_2$ is the most recent Executive Compensation and Exec. Comp.$_1$ is Executive Compensation in the prior year.

Suppose Executive Compensation was $700,000 this year and $620,000 last year. What is the Growth in Exec. Compensation?

$$= \frac{\$700,000 - \$620,000}{\$620,000}$$

$$= 12.9\%$$

Growth in CEO compensation

The Growth in CEO Compensation is similar to the growth in Executive Compensation except that it singles out the CEO as shown in equation (7.5). The reason for focusing special attention on the CEO is that she or he is usually in the best position to influence his or her compensation independent of the company's performance.

$$\text{Growth in CEO Compensation} = \frac{\text{CEO Comp}_2 - \text{CEO Comp}_1}{\text{CEO Comp}_1} \qquad (7.5)$$

Where CEO Comp$_2$ is the most recent CEO Compensation and CEO Comp$_1$ is CEO Compensation in the prior year.

Suppose a CEO was compensated $300,000 this year and $275,000 last year. What is the Growth in CEO Compensation?

$$= \frac{\$300,000 - \$275,000}{\$275,000}$$

$$= 9.1\%$$

Growth in executive compensation to Growth in EBITDA

The purpose of this ratio is to see whether executives are generating new value faster than they are harvesting value for themselves. This requires comparing the Growth in Executive Compensation to the Growth in EBITDA as shown in equation (7.6)

$$\frac{\text{Growth in Exec. Compensation}}{\text{to Growth in EBITDA}} = \frac{\text{Growth in Exec. Compensation}}{\text{Growth in EBITDA}} \qquad (7.6)$$

Suppose EBITDA is growing at 7.0% per year and Executive Compensation Growth is 12.9% per year. What is the ratio?

$$= 12.9\% / 7\%$$

$$= 1.84$$

A ratio of 1.0 means Executive Compensation and EBITDA are growing at the same rate. A ratio higher than 1.0 means executives are harvesting value from the company faster than they are creating it. This should be a danger sign to a board of directors or an investor. A ratio substantially less than 1.0 means management is growing value faster than it is appropriating it.

Ownership multiples

To align management's interest with that of the shareholders, some companies require the CEO and other senior managers to own some multiple of their salary in company stock. For example for 2008, Campbell Soup required the following ownership;

	CEO	6.0 times base salary
	CEO Direct Reports	3.5 times base salary
	Other Participating Executives	2.0 times base salary

Approximately 35 executives were required to own company stock.[1]

Executive bonuses

Some executive bonuses are based on achievement of key ratios. For example, General Electric's bonuses are based on achieving target growth in (i) EPS, (ii) revenue, (iii) return on assets, and (iv) cash flow from operations. To encourage long term sustainable strategies and prevent short term manipulation of these key ratios, measurements are based on a three year average. All four ratios are weighted equally.[2] Other companies use different ratios. Each company sets its own targets for ratio improvement. Most targets range from 10% to 15% per year.

Suppose a company's management incentive program was based on increasing Earnings per Share (EPS), Revenue, Return on Assets, and Cash Flow from Operations an average of 12% per year over a three year average. If all targets are met, the executive can get a bonus equal to 100% of his or her salary. Each performance goal is worth 25% of the potential bonus so the total bonus could be computed using equation (7.7). Assume that exceeding a goal provides no additional compensation.

Suppose an executive had a base salary of $200,000 and a potential bonus of up to an additional $200,000 if all goals were met. Given the following information compute the executive's bonus.

	Base Year	Year 1	Year 2	Year 3	3 Year Average	Percent of Target
EPS	$1.00	$1.08	$1.18	$1.30		
EPS Growth		*8.0%*	*9.3%*	*10.2%*	*9.2%*	*76.7%*
Revenue	$50M	$55M	$60M	$64M		
Revenue Growth		*10%*	*9.1%*	*6.7%*	*8.6%*	*71.7%*
Return on Assets	7.0%	7.8%	8.2%	8.8%		
ROA Growth		*11.4%*	*5.1%*	*7.3%*	*7.9%*	*66.1%*
Cash Flow from Operations	$4M	$5M	$6M	$7M		
Cash Flow Growth		*25.0%*	*20.0%*	*16.7%*	*20.6%*	*100.0%*

---

1 *Campbell Soup. 2008. Schedule 14A, Proxy Statement Pursuant to Section 14(a) of the SEA off 1934. October 9.*

2 *General Electric. 2008. Schedule 14A Proxy Statement Pursuant to Section 14(a) of the SEA of 1934. April 23.*

Bonus= Base Salary x (.25 x %EPS Target   (7.7)

    + .25 x %Revenue Target

        + .25 x %ROA Target

            + .25 x %Cash Flow from Operations Target)

= $200,000 x (.25 x 76.7% + .25 x 71.7% + .25 x 66.1% + .25 x 100%)

= $200,000 x (19.2% + 17.9% + 16.5% + 25.0%)

 = $200,000 x 78.6%

= $157,200

Bonus plans can also be structured so that an executive must meet at least 50% of each target or there is no contribution from that component of the compensation. For example, suppose EPS only increased by 5% per year on average, the contribution on this component would be zero and the percentage applied to the potential bonus would only be 59.4% (0.0% + 17.9% + 16.5% + 25%) reducing the bonus to $118,800.

Options

An option is the right to purchase a stock for a stated price some time in the future. Companies award management options to align management's interest with that of shareholders. Arguably if management's actions increase share price, shareholders benefit, and managers also benefit through the options. Replacing interest with growth rate enables us to use a modified version of the future value formula to estimate the target value shares should reach for management to benefit. See equation (7.8).

$$FV= PV \times (1 + g)^n \qquad (7.8)$$

Where FV is the future target value of the shares, PV is the present value of the shares, g is the target growth rate and n is the number of years over which management incentive plan works. FV will become the strike price for the incentive plan options. If management can drive the stock price higher than the strike price, they can profit from the options.

Suppose a company's stock price is $10 per share and the board wants management to increase share price at least 15% per year for three years. What should the strike price be?

= $10 x (1 + 15%)^3

= $10 x 1.521

= $15.21

Suppose a manager is awarded 10,000 options, with a strike price of $15.21, which vests in three years (vesting is when a person earns the legal right to something). Suppose the market price of the stock is $21.00. The value of the compensation at vesting is $57,900. This is the difference between the cost at the option price of $152,100 ($15.21 x 10,000) and the value at which the stock can be sold $210,000 ($21.00 x 10,000).

Severance

Executives often negotiate for, and Boards approve, severance pay. Severance for cause, can result in little or no compensation. However, severance compensation can be triggered by retirement or voluntary resignation. Sometimes severance for cause is characterized as a voluntary resignation to avoid litigation.

Severance compensation can include equity, health and welfare benefits and cash. If a CEO or other executive is doing a poor job, but not stealing from the company or behaving unethically and the company determines it must let him or her go, that is usually classified as severance without cause. Most CEOs are under contract for a specified length of time. An alternative to termination is non-renewal of the contract. Whether this results in severance compensation will be found in the details of the contract.

Another kind of severance compensation occurs when there is a change in the control of a company. This usually occurs when the company is bought out by another company. There is a substantial question as to whether severance packages benefit shareholders.

Conclusion

The primary issue in executive compensation are whether executives are taking a disproportionate amount of shareholder wealth. The ratios of sales, EBITDA and Net Income to executive compensation are a fairly sensitive ways to determine whether executives are taking progressively more of shareholder wealth. These ratios must be compared over time to identify trends. The year to year growth in executive compensation, CEO compensation and the change in CEO compensation relative to the growth of EBITDA provide other ways to judge the reasonableness of executive compensation.

Several schemes have been tried to align executive interests with those of shareholders. Some companies require executives to own some multiple of their salary in company stock. Some companies link bonuses to achievement of certain key ratios. Other companies try to align executive interests with those of shareholders by awarding options which will only have value if executives substantially increase share price.

Most executives negotiate severance packages. If an executive is terminated for cause, stealing or unethical conduct, the executive might get nothing. However, if an executive is merely underperforming, the board may terminate the executive and pay a predetermined severance. Severance can also be triggered by the retirement or voluntary resignation of an executive, or by a change in company control. Severance packages can include cash, stock, and benefits such as health insurance and pension benefits. There is a substantial question as to whether severance packages benefit shareholders.

CHAPTER 8

Break Even Analysis and Profit Modeling

Introduction

Generally Accepted Accounting Principals (GAAP) require use of Full Absorption Costing (FAC) for cost of goods sold and inventory valuation. GAAP is concerned with historical reporting. Management accounting focuses on improving management decisions. One element of management accounting is variable costing which asks questions like, how do costs and profits change with production volume, what if fixed costs are substituted for variable costs, and how much of a safety margin does the company have if sales decline? Flexibility in the design and use of variable costing makes management accounting a very powerful decision making tool.

Full absorption cost versus variable costing

Full Absorption Cost (FAC) includes direct materials (DM), direct labor (DL), variable factory overhead (VFOH) and fixed factory overhead (FFOH) as shown in equation (8.1).

$$FAC = DM + DL + VFOH + FFOH \qquad (8.1)$$

Variable factory overhead includes things like heat, electricity, water, miscellaneous shop supplies and factory labor which is hard to trace into a particular product such as the wages for warehouse and maintenance operations. Fixed factory overhead includes things like the cost of the factory building, plant manager's salary and depreciation. Variable overhead drops to zero when the factory stops producing. Fixed factory costs are incurred whether ten units are produced, a thousand units or zero units.

Suppose a company uses $10 of direct material, $8 of direct labor, $2 of variable factory overhead, fixed factory overhead is $20,000 and the plant plans to build 8,000 units. Fixed factory overhead cannot be allocated to a product until an estimate of production is made. In this case, $20,000 of fixed factory overhead will be allocated across 8,000 units for a fixed factory overhead charge of $2.50 per unit ($20,000 / 8,000). What is the full absorption cost of a unit?

FAC= $10 + $8 + $2 + $2.50

= $22.50

Gross Margin – Product Level

While Gross Margin is usually computed at a company level, it can also be computed at a product level as shown in equation (8.2). Price is substituted for sales and the full absorption cost of the product is substituted for COGS. Gross margin is the percent of every dollar that is left over for overhead, financing costs, taxes and profits after a product is made.

$$\text{Product Gross Margin} = \frac{\text{Price} - \text{FAC}}{\text{Price}} \qquad (8.2)$$

Suppose a product has a price of $30 and full absorption cost of $22.50. What is its Product Gross Margin?

$$= \frac{\$30.00 - \$22.50}{\$30.00}$$

= 25%

Gross Margin is always quoted as a percentage. A company's overall gross margin is the weighted average of individual product gross margins. Companies should periodically assess the gross margin of its products and eliminate those with low, or negative gross margins. Eliminating low performing products will free up working capital, plant, equipment and management time for more profitable products.

Customer Profitability

As a general rule, 80% of sales and profits will come from 20% of customers. Just as some products have a better gross margin or contribution than other products, some customers are more profitable than others. Customer profitability is a combination of the profitability of the products a customer buys, the volume purchased and a number of period costs that can be traced to individual customers. Customers should be routinely analyzed for profitability and low profit or no profit customers should be dropped.

Cost per Sales Order

Suppose a company has two customers each of which order 10,000 units of the same good per year. Are they equally profitable? If one customer places 100 orders for 100 units each and the other customer places four orders for 2,500 units each they are not equally profitable.

For each order placed, costs are incurred for order entry, production scheduling, expediting and customer service, routine billing and collection. An individual order cost can be estimated using equation (8.3).

$$\text{Order Cost} = \frac{\begin{array}{c}\text{Order Entry Salaries \& Expenses}\\ + \text{Expeditor \& Customer Service Salaries \& Expenses}\\ + \text{Routine Billing \& Collection Salaries Expenses}\end{array}}{\text{Number of Orders}} \qquad (8.3)$$

Suppose a company has three order entry clerks at a salary of $35,000 each, other order entry expenses for computers and supplies is $20,000; there are three expeditor/customer service representatives with a salary of $60,000 each and other customer service costs are $25,000; and routine billing and collection costs are $80,000. The company processes 2,000 orders per year. What is the Cost per Order?

$$= \frac{3 \times \$35,000 + \$20,000 + 3 \times \$60,000 + \$25,000 + \$80,000}{2,000}$$

$$= \$410,000 / 2,000$$

$$= \$205$$

Slow Pay Cost

Most customers promptly pay their bills. However, there are a handful of customers that always pay late, claim they have lost the invoice or otherwise need special collection attention. This extra collection cost should be considered when trying to decide which customers are profitable. Billing and collections should know who these customers are, but one way to identify them is through a simple aging. If most customers pay within 30 days, prepare a list of all those with accounts receivable more than 45 days old to identify slow pay customers. If one fifth of billing and collections time (20%) is spent with slow-pay customers, then one fifth of billing and collection costs should be allocated to those customers as shown in equation (8.4).

$$\text{Slow Pay Cost} = \frac{20\% \times (\text{Billing \& Collection Salaries} + \text{Other Billing \& Collection Expenses})}{\text{Number of Slow Pay Customers}} \qquad (8.4)$$

Suppose a company has billing and collection salaries of $85,000; other billing and collection expenses of $15,000; and 20 slow pay customers.

$$= \frac{20\% \times (\$85,000 + \$15,000)}{20}$$

$$= \$1,000$$

Customer Account Maintenance

A certain amount of time and attention must be expended just to keep an account open. For some companies that means in-person sales calls, for others it might mean phone calls, mailings, or writing proposals. The exact costs to maintain a customer account will vary from industry to industry. Most of the costs of maintaining a customer account can be found in the selling and marketing budget. An estimate of the costs to maintain a customer account is shown in equation (8.5).

$$\text{Customer Act Cost} = \frac{\text{Salespersons' Base Salaries} + \text{Travel} + \text{Phone Expenses} + \text{Proposals}}{\text{Number of Customers}} \qquad (8.5)$$

Suppose salespersons' base salaries are $105,000; travel is $15,000; phone expenses are $8,000 and the cost to write proposals is $12,000. Writing proposals usually includes more than salespersons' effort. It often includes cost accounting, engineering, and if a company has estimators, estimators. Suppose a company has 120 customers. What is the cost of maintaining the average customer account?

$$= \frac{\$105,000 + \$15,000 + \$8,000 + \$12,000}{120}$$

= $140,000 / 120

= $1,167

Special Packaging & Handling

Some customers require special packaging and handling. Early in the last century Ford required all parts be shipped in wooden boxes of a certain size so it could use the box boards for flooring in its Model T automobiles. Wal-Mart now requires all suppliers to send material packaged with RFID chips. Special Packaging & Handling is a customer specific cost for which there is no ratio.

Shipping

Shipping is not an issue if the customer pays shipping. However, if the company pays shipping, those costs should be captured to determine customer profitability. It costs far less on a per unit basis to ship 5,000 units rather than 1 unit. If it is impractical to trace shipping costs back to individual customers, shipping costs can be roughly estimated by dividing total shipping costs by the number of orders as shown in equation (8.6). It is better to track exact shipping costs if practical.

$$\text{Shipping Cost} = \frac{\text{Total Shipping Costs}}{\text{Number of Orders}} \qquad (8.6)$$

Suppose a company has $360,000 of shipping costs and 2,000 orders. What is the average shipping cost?

= $360,000 / 2,000

= $180

Customer Profitability

The elements of customer profitability can be combined as shown in equation (8,7).

$$\text{Customer. Profitability} = \text{Sales x Gross Margin} - n \text{ x Order Cost} \qquad (8.7)$$
$$- \text{ Slow Pay Cost}$$
$$- \text{ Customer Act. Maintenance}$$
$$- \text{ Special Packaging \& Handling}$$
$$- n \text{ x Shipping}$$

Consider the profitability of just three of a company's customers using the data in Table 8-1 Customer Profitability and assuming each unit of product has a gross margin of 35%, the company pays the shipping, and the ratios above apply.

	Sales	Gross Profit	Orders	Order Cost	Slow Pay	Account Main- tenance	Special Hand- ling	Shipping	Customer Profit
Alice Co.	$1,000,000	$350,000	100	$20,500	-	$1,167	-	$18,000	$310,333
Bob Co.	$1,000,000	$350,000	4	$820	-	$1,167	-	$720	$347,293
Sam Co.	$50,000	$17,500	40	$8,200	$1,000	$1,167	-	$7,200	- $67

In this example, it can be seen that customers are less profitable if they order small quantities or are slow pay customers. Low or no profit customers consume a disproportionate share of management time and attention and should be eliminated so the company can focus on developing higher profit customers.

Variable Cost

Variable costs are the incremental costs of making and selling one additional unit. Variable costs include direct material (DM), direct labor (DL), variable factory overhead (VFOH), variable selling costs (VSC), and variable administrative costs (VAC) as shown in equation (8.8). Commissions are a prime example of a variable selling cost. Credit checks are an example of a variable administrative cost.

$$\text{Variable Cost} = DM + DL + VFOH + VSC + VAC \qquad (8.8)$$

Suppose direct material is $10, direct labor is $8, variable factory overhead is $2, variable selling cost is $3 and fixed factory overhead is $2.50. What is the variable selling cost for a unit of this product?

$$= \$10 + \$8 + \$2 + \$3$$

$$= \$23$$

Notice that fixed factory overhead is not part of variable cost. Why? Because it's fixed!

Contribution

Contribution is an estimate of how much is left to cover fixed costs after variable costs are covered. Contribution is the difference between sales and variable costs as shown in equation (8.9). Contribution is a building block for modeling a company's performance and forecasting profits.

$$\text{Contribution} = \text{Sales} - \text{Variable Costs} \qquad (8.9)$$

Suppose a company has $20 million of sales and variable costs of $13 million. What is its contribution?

$$= \$20 \text{ million} - \$13 \text{ million}$$

$$= \$7 \text{ million}$$

Contribution – Product Level

Contribution can be computed at the product level as the difference between selling price and variable cost as shown by equation (8.10).

$$\text{Product Contribution} = \text{Price} - \text{Variable Cost} \qquad (8.10)$$

Suppose a product has a price of $30 and a variable cost of $23. What is its contribution?

$$= \$30 - \$23$$

$$= \$7$$

Contribution Margin

A company's contribution margin is the percent of every dollar of sales that contributes to covering fixed costs. The formula for contribution margin is given in equation (8.11).

$$\text{Contribution Margin} = \frac{\text{Sales} - \text{Variable Costs}}{\text{Sales}} \qquad (8.11)$$

Suppose a company has sales of $20 million and variable costs of $13 million. What is its Contribution Margin?

$$= \frac{\$20 \text{ million} - \$13 \text{ million}}{\$20 \text{ million}}$$

$$= \$7 \text{ million} / \$20 \text{ million}$$

$$= 35\%$$

Contribution Margin is always stated as a percentage.

Contribution Margin – Product Level

Contribution Margin may be computed at a product level by substituting Price for Sales and the variable cost of a particular product for the variable costs of the company as shown in equation (8.12).

$$\text{Product Contribution Margin} = \frac{\text{Price} - \text{Variable Costs}}{\text{Price}} \tag{8.12}$$

Suppose a product is priced at $30 and variable costs are $23. What is its Contribution Margin?

$$= \frac{\$30 - \$23}{\$30}$$

$$= \$7 / \$30$$

$$= 23.3\%$$

A company's overall contribution margin is the weighted average of individual product contribution margins. Companies should periodically analyze product contribution and eliminate products with low or no contribution.

Operating Leverage

Operating Leverage is a tool used to model how net income changes with sales. Operating Leverage is contribution divided by operating income as shown in equation (8.13). Operating income is income generated by operations. It is pre-tax, pre-financing cost income.

$$\text{Operating Leverage} = \frac{\text{Contribution}}{\text{Operating Income}} \tag{8.13}$$

Suppose a company has a contribution of $4 million and operating income of $1.5 million. What is its operating leverage?

$$= \$4 \text{ million} / \$1.5 \text{ million}$$

$$= 2.67$$

Operating Leverage is always quoted as a dimensionless number.

Modeling Profit with Operating Leverage

Operating Leverage can be used to link a percentage change in sales to a percentage change in net income as shown in equation (8.14).

$$\%\Delta \text{ Operating Income} = \text{Operating Leverage} \times \%\Delta \text{ Sales} \tag{8.14}$$

Where the symbol Δ means change. Suppose a company has an Operating Leverage of 2.67 and sales increase 7%. How much should operating income increase?

= 2.67 x 7%

= 18.69%

Operating Leverage can be used to forecast the change in profits whether sales increase or decrease. When the economy is expanding, and sales are rising, a company wants a high operating leverage, but when the economy tips into a recession, as it does from time to time, a company wants a low operating leverage.

Operating leverage can be changed by changing the mix of costs that go into a product. For example, machines which represent fixed costs, can be substituted for labor which is a variable cost. At the beginning of an expansion a company wants low variable costs, which increase the contribution, and relatively higher fixed costs which remain the same as production increases. But during an economic downturn, a company should want its costs to be variable rather than fixed so it can easily contract to profitably serve a smaller sales base.

Break Even Analysis

Classical break even analysis asks the question, how may units of a product must be made and sold to cover fixed costs. Classical break even analysis does not contemplate profits. The formula for break even analysis is given in equation (8.15). Using algebra to factor out units provides a more useful version of the formula as shown in equation (8.16).

$$0 = \text{Price x Units} - \text{Variable Cost x Units} - \text{Fixed Costs} \qquad (8.15)$$

$$= (\text{Price} - \text{Variable Costs}) \times \text{Units} - \text{Fixed Costs} \qquad (8.16)$$

No plant manager is going to keep his or her job very long if she or he tells corporate headquarters their plan is to break even. Corporate will demand profits. From the point of view of the plant manager, his or her profit target becomes another fixed cost. This is an extension of classical break even analysis in which equation (8.16) is rewritten as equation (8.17) to include profit targets.

$$0 = (\text{Price} - \text{Variable Costs}) \times \text{Units} - \text{Fixed Costs} - \text{Target Profits} \qquad (8.17)$$

Suppose a product has a price of $30, variable costs of $23, fixed costs for the plant are $100,000 per month, and the target profit is $50,000 per month. How many units must the company make and sell to meet its goals?

= ($30 - $23) x Units - $100,000 - $50,000

= $7 x Units - $150,000

$150,000= \$7$ x Units

$150,000 / \$7=$ Units

$= 21,429$ Units

The answer is in units. The actual calculation gives the answer of 21,428.57, but since it is difficult to make a fractional unit, the number must be rounded up to 21,429 to make sure the plant meets its goal.

Margin of Safety

Margin of safety is a way to determine whether a company is robust or just barely making its goals. This measure is particularly important when an economic downturn is forecast or new competitors are, or could, take away market share.

Margin of Safety in Units

The margin of safety in units is the number of units by which sales exceed the classical break even of equation (8.15). The margin of safety in units is given by equation (8.18).

Margin of Safety in Units= Units Sold – Break even Units   (8.18)

Suppose a company has sales of 23,000 units, the price per unit is \$30, variable costs are \$23, and fixed costs are \$100,000. Using equation (8.15) we find classical break even is

$0= (\$30 - \$23)$ x Units - $\$100,000$

$\$100,000= \$7$ x Units

$\$100,000 / \$7=$ Units $= 14,286$ Units

Using equation (8.18) the margin of safety is

$= 23,000$ Units $– 14,286$ Units

$= 8,714$

Margin of Safety Dollars

Margin of Safety can also be expressed in dollars as shown in equation (8.19)

Margin of Safety\$= Sales – Break Even Sales   (8.19)

Suppose sales are 23,000 units of a product priced at \$30 and classical break even is 14,286 units. What is the Margin of Safety in dollars?

$= \$30$ x $23,000 - \$30$ x $14,286$

= $690,000 - $428.580

= $261,420

In this example, sales could decline by $261,420 and the company would still be able to cover its fixed costs. Of course with such a sales decline there would be no profits. The reason for expressing margin of safety in dollars is that most people conceptualize sales goals in terms of dollars not units.

Margin of Safety as a Percent

Margin of Safety can be expressed as a percent. It is the Margin of Safety divided by classical break even as shown in equation (8.20). This equation works equally well whether the margin of safety and break even are expressed in units or in dollars. However, one cannot mix units and dollars.

Margin of Safety%= Margin of Safety / Break Even   (8.20)

Suppose a company had sales of 23,000 units and a Margin of Safety of 8,714 units. What is its Margin of Safety%?

= 8,714 / 23,000

= 37.0%

Margin of Safety% is always stated as a percent. It is a way of quantifying how close to the edge a company is. For example, a margin of safety of 5% would indicate a company is barely breaking even and even a small sales decline could tip it over into losses. A margin of safety of 37.9% means there would have to be a 37.9% sales decline for a company to incur an operating loss.

Had the margin of safety been computed in dollars, and assuming the price of every unit were $30, the Margin of Safety$ would have been $261,420 and sales would have been $690,000 giving a Margin of Safety% of 37.9% ($261,420 / $690,000).

Note that the Margin of Safety% in units and in dollars only are only equal when a company has a single product. If a company has multiple products, the Margin of Safety% in units has no meaning for the company as a whole.

Break Even Multiple Products

While a single plant may have a single product. Few companies have a single product which makes it difficult to apply either classical or extended break even analysis. A company trying to analyze its competitors is further handicapped because competitors rarely disclose details about fixed and variable costs. On the other hand, published financial data can be used to estimate fixed and variable costs.

Let cost of goods sold be an estimate of variable costs. This isn't a perfect estimate because one element of cost of goods sold is fixed factory overhead. Nevertheless it is useful. Let overhead and financing costs be estimates of fixed costs. Financing costs are hard to change over the short run and overhead shouldn't rise or fall in direct proportion to sales. Adapting equation (8.15), replace Price x Units with Sales; replace Variable Costs x Units with COGS; and replace Fixed Costs with Overhead and Financing Costs to get equation (8.21).

0= Sales – COGS – Overhead – Financing Costs   (8.21)

Substituting (1- Gross Margin) x Sales for COGS gives equation (8.22) and factoring out Sales give equation (8.23).

0= Sales – (1 –Gross Margin) x Sales –Overhead –Financing Costs   (8.22)

0= Sales x Gross Margin – Overhead – Financing Costs   (8.23)

Suppose a company has a Gross Margin of 35%, Overhead of $5 million and Financing Costs of $1 million. What sales does it need to break even?

0= Sales x 35% - $5 million - $1 million

$6 million = Sales x 35%

$6 million /35%= Sales

= $17.14 million

Lowering overhead or financing costs will lower the sales needed to break even. A Profit Target can be treated as another fixed cost as shown by modifying equation (8.23) to get equation (8.24).

0= Sales x Gross Margin – Overhead – Financing Costs -Target Profit   (8.24)

This equation can be used to analyze competitors or to determine Overhead, Gross Margin and Sales needed to reach a pre-tax Target Profit.

Suppose a company has a Gross Margin of 35%, Overhead of $5 million, Financing Costs of $1 million, and a Target Profit of $2 million. What sales does it need?

0= Sales x 35% - $5 million - $1 million - $2 million

$8 million= Sales x 35%

$8 million /35%= Sales

= $22.86 million

Reverse Engineering Profits

Sales are usually the hardest thing to control. A company should determine how to restructure itself to make its profit target within the bounds of expected sales. Building on equation (8.24) one can forecast the Required sales using a given mix of Other Overhead, Financing Costs, Gross Margin, Selling Cost% and Target profit. Recall that Overhead can be split into Selling and Marketing expenses, which are expected to rise and fall with sales and Other Overhead which is not expected to rise and fall with sales. Selling Cost% is Selling and Marketing Costs divided by Sales. If Required Sales are greater than forecast sales a company must rethink its cost model until Required Sales is less than or equal to forecast sales.

$$\text{Required Sales} = \frac{\text{Other Overhead} + \text{Financing Costs} + \text{Target Profit}}{(\text{Gross Margin} - \text{Selling Cost\%})} \qquad (8.25)$$

Suppose a company has Other Overhead of $4 million, Financing Costs of $1 million, Target Profit of $2 million, Gross Margin of 35%, Selling Cost% of 4%, and forecast sales of $21 million. What are Required Sales and will forecast sales be enough to carry the company's cost structure and Profit Target?

$$= \frac{\$4 \text{ million} + \$1 \text{ million} + \$2 \text{ million}}{(35\% - 4\%)}$$

$$= \$7 \text{ million} / 31\%$$

$$= \$22.6 \text{ million}$$

This company will fall short of its goals because forecast sales of $21 million is less than the sales required to carry its cost structure and target profits. Suppose the company cut Other Overhead by $0.8 million and increased its Gross Margin by 1%.

$$= \frac{\$3.2 \text{ million} + \$1 \text{ million} + \$2 \text{ million}}{(36\% - 4\%)}$$

$$= \$6.2 \text{ million} / 32\%$$

$$= \$19.4 \text{ million}$$

In this example a company will meet it goals because required sales of $19.4 million is less than forecast sales of $21 million.. Equation (8.25) along with a sales forecast can be used to model and set overarching performance targets for the whole company. Reverse engineering target profits adds realism to annual plans.

Conclusion

Ratios and related equations can be used to estimate how profits change with sales, costs and production volume. Generally Accepted Accounting Principals (GAAP) is historical in nature and is used to value cost of goods sold. Cost of goods sold is used to compute gross margin. If a company's gross margin is too small, it will not make enough money to cover overhead, financing costs, taxes and profit. Gross margin can be computed at the product level as well as company level. A company's gross margin is simply the weighted average gross margin for its products.

Customer profitability can be estimated by tracing or allocating non-product costs to particular customers. Examples of costs that can be traced to customers include order costs, costs to keep an account open, slow pay costs, shipping and special handling costs.

Variable costing segregates fixed and variable costs. It is not bound by the strictures of historical GAAP accounting. Rather, it is used to model the outcome of proposed or expected sales, cost and production volumes.

Contribution is the amount by which sales exceed variable costs. Contribution can be computed at the company or product level. The company contribution margin is contribution divided by sales. Product contribution margin is product level divided by price. The company contribution margin is the weighted average of product contributions. Leverage is a ratio that shows the relationship between contribution and operating income.

Classical break even analysis determines the number of units to exactly cover fixed and variable costs. Break even analysis can be extended to cover profits by treating them as another fixed cost. Safety margin is the amount by which a company's sales exceeds classical break even.

It is often useful to analyze competitor's financial statements when setting goals or looking for their strategic weaknesses. Unfortunately few companies are willing to publish their fixed and variable costs. Extended break-even can be adapted by using cost of goods sold as an estimate of variable costs and overhead and financing costs as estimates of fixed costs. These estimates are imperfect because cost of goods sold contains some fixed costs.

Sales, and various categories of expenses can be used to reverse engineer how to achieve target profits. If the sales required to cover costs and target profits is greater than forecast sales, a company's cost structure must be re-worked until the company finds a combination of sales and costs that will allow it to reach its target profits. Reverse engineering target profits adds realism to annual plans.

CHAPTER 9

Time Value of Money

Introduction

The value of money changes over time.; $1,000 today is worth more than $1,000 to be received in a year or ten years. The changing value of money creates problems for individuals who must make decisions in the here and now that will result in the payment or receipt of money in the future.

The time value of money is used to value bonds and notes, savings, to rank capital investments, determine car and mortgage payments, and measure growth rates. Considering the time value of money adds another level of sophistication to financial analysis.

Interest and Discount Rates

Interest is the payment received for the use of money. For example when a customer purchases a certificate of deposit, the bank pays the customer interest for use of his or her money. How much the bank pays is a function of several factors including how badly it wants the money and what other banks are paying. The amount of interest a borrower pays is a function of how badly the borrower needs the money, the cost of money from other sources and the creditworthiness of the borrower.

With interest one starts with a known amount of money and projects how much money one with have in the future. A discount rate is used where one knows the amount to be received in the future and one wants to know what that is worth in today's dollars. A discount rate can be thought of as sandpaper wearing away the value of money. The courser the sandpaper (the higher the discount rate) and the longer the time, the more the value of money will be worn away.

The discount rate is based on (i) the risk free rate of return which is usually estimated as the rate on a one year treasury bill, plus (ii) the maturity risk premium, that is the risk of inflation over time, plus (iii) the default risk premium which is risk that the payer won't or can't pay what is owed, plus (iv) the liquidity risk premium, that is the difficulty in selling the investment. One can always find a buyer for treasury bills so the liquidity risk premium is zero for government bonds. However, it might be difficult to find a buyer for a bond issued by Bob's Autoworld located on the Admiral Wilson Boulevard in Camden.

The easiest way to estimate the appropriate discount rate is to look at the rate charged on bonds of similar risk. The discount rate, market rate and the yield on a bond are the same thing. Bond yields are published in the *Wall Street Journal*.

Future Value

Future value is the number of dollars that will be generated by investing a certain amount of dollars, at a given interest rate, for a certain period of time. Future value can be computed using equation (9.1).

$$FV = PV \times (1 + i)^n \qquad (9.1)$$

Where FV is the value to be received in the future. PV is the present value of the amount invested in today's dollars, i is the period interest rate and n is the number of periods over which the investment is compounded.

Suppose $7,500 is invested at 5% interest for six years. What is the future value of this investment?

$$= \$7{,}500 \times (1 + 5\%)^6$$
$$= \$7{,}500 \times 1.3401$$
$$= \$10{,}050.75$$

Compounding

In the prior example interest was computed and added to the initial investment once per year. However, interest is sometimes computed (compounded) more than once per year. To work out problems where there is multiple compounding the period interest rate, i, and the number of periods, n, must be adjusted using equations (9.2) and (9.3).

Period interest rate $i =$ Annual interest rate / Number of periods in a year   (9.2)

Number of periods $n =$ Number of years x Number of periods in a year   (9.3)

Suppose 5% annual percentage rate (APR) is compounded monthly (12 times per year) for six years. What is the period interest rate i, and the number of periods n?

$i = $ 5% APR / 12 periods per year

$$= 0.4167\%$$

n= 6 years x 12 periods per year

$$= 72$$

If the initial investment is $7,500, what is the future value?

$$= \$7,500 \times (1 + 0.4167\%)^{72}$$

$$= \$7,500 \times 1.3490$$

$$= \$10,117.50$$

In this example, monthly compounding increases interest earned by $66.75 ($10,117.50 - $10,050.75) or about 2.6% ($66.75 / $2,550.75 interest).

Present Value

Present value is the value in today's dollars of an amount to be received in the future. Equation (9.4) can be used to compute present value.

$$PV = \frac{FV}{(1 + k)^n} \qquad (9.4)$$

Suppose a company offers you a $50,000 bonus if you stay with the company for three years. What is it worth in today's dollars? Before you can answer this question, you must select a discount rate. If the company has bonds, you can use the yield on those bonds as the discount rate. If it doesn't have bonds, find a company of similar risk and use their yield as a discount rate. Suppose the discount rate for your employer is 18%. What is the present value of the $50,000 bonus?

$$= \$50,000 / (1 + 18\%)^3$$

$$= \$50,000 / 1.64303$$

$$= \$30,431.58$$

As a general rule, where there is only one payment to be received at the end of a period of time, amounts are discounted annually.

Future Value of an Annuity

An annuity is an even stream of payments. An annuity can be a stream of payments coming in, or a stream of payments going out.

The future value of an annuity is the amount that would accumulate if one saved the same amount every period and invested that money at interest. The future value of an annuity is given in equation (9.5).

$$FV = Payment \times \frac{(1 + i)^n - 1}{i} \tag{9.5}$$

Where Payment is the periodic payment, i is the period interest rate and n is the number of periods over which payments are made.

Suppose a person saved $1,000 per month for five years and invested it at an annual percentage rate of 6%. How much would they have?

First compute the period interest rate, i, using equation (9.2).

i= 6% annual percentage rate / 12 periods per year

= 0.5%

Next compute the number of periods using equation (9.3).

n= 5 years x 12 periods per year

= 60

Then compute the future value of the annuity.

$$= \$1,000 \times \frac{(1 + 0.5\%)^{60} - 1}{0.5\%}$$

$$= \$1,000 \times \frac{(1.34885 - 1)}{.005}$$

$$= \$1,000 \times 69.77003$$

$$= \$69,770.03$$

Present Value of an Annuity

The present value of an annuity is the value in present dollars of an even stream of payments to be received in the future. The present value of an annuity can be computed using equation (9.6).

$$PV = Payment \times [1/k - (1/k) \times (1 / (1 + k)^n] \tag{9.6}$$

Where PV is the present value of the annuity, Payment is the amount paid each period, k is the period discount rate and n is the number of periods.

Suppose someone wants to buy a piece of land and offers $600 per month for eight years. How much are they really offering? To make the calculation, one must find or estimate a discount rate. The riskier the buyer, the higher the discount rate that should be used. The discount rate should be at least the current rate on mortgages, and probably not more that three times that rate. Suppose a discount rate of 15% per year is selected. First compute the period interest rate by adapting equation (9.2) to get (9.7).

k= Annual Discount Rate / Number of periods per year   (9.7)

= 15% / 12 payments per year

= 1.25%

Then compute the number of periods using equation (9.3).

Number of periods n= Number of years x Number of periods in a year   (9.3)

= 8 years x 12 payments per year

= 96

PV= $600 x [(1 / 1.25%) − (1 / 1.25%) x (1 / (1 +1.25%)^{96})]

= $600 x [80 − 80 x (1 / 3.29551)]

= $600 x [80 − 24.27545]

= $600 x 55.72455

= $33,434.73

This is significantly less than the $57,600 of checks that will be received ($600 per month times 96 months). The difference can be thought of as interest paid to finance the purchase.

Functions

A function is a mathematical machine. It is a shorthand way of representing an equation. A function is a machine in which inputs are put in the top, a crank is turned and a result comes out. The future value can be written in functional notation as shown in equation (9.4).

FVIF(i, n)= $(1 + i)^n$ (9.8)

In functional notation FVIF(i, n) is read as the future value interest factor at i period interest for n periods.

Present value can be written in functional notation as shown in equation (9.9)

$$PVIF(k, n)= \frac{FV}{(1 + k)^n}$$ (9.9)

The present valuation function can be read as the present value interest factor at k period discount for n periods.

The future value of an annuity formula can be written as a function as shown in equation (9.10).

$$FVIFA(i, n) = \frac{(1 + i)^n - 1}{i} \qquad (9.10)$$

This function can be read as the future value interest factor of an annuity at i period interest rate for n periods.

The present value of an annuity can be written as shown in equation (9.11).

$$PVIFA(k, n) = [\, 1/k - (1/k) \times (1 / (1 + k)^n)\,] \qquad (9.11)$$

This function can be read as the present value interest factor of an annuity at k period discount rate for n periods.

Tables

Once a problem has been written in functional notation it is often possible to estimate the answer using pre-printed tables. These tables have selectively computed values for Future Value (Appendix A), Present Value (Appendix B), Future Value Interest Factor for an Annuity (Appendix C) and Present Value Interest Factor for an Annuity (Appendix D) for common values of i, k, and n.

Suppose one wants to compute the future value of $7,500 invested at 5% annual percentage rate (APR) for six years, compounded monthly. The period interest rate is 0.4167% (5% APR / 12 months per year) and the number of periods, is 72 (6 years x 12 months per year.) Then we can use equation (9.8) write the problem in functional notation as shown in equation (9.12).

$$FV = PV \times FVIF(i, n) \qquad (9.12)$$

$$= \$7,500 \times FVIF(0.4167\%, 72)$$

Using the Future Value Interest Factor table, Appendix A, read down the left side to n equals 72, then read across to the column headed by 0.4167%. to find 1.3490 which is FVIF(0.4167%, 72).

$$= \$7,500 \times 1.3490$$

$$= \$10,117.50$$

Loans

Computing Loan Payments

One of the most common uses for the present value of an annuity function is to compute loan payments. Rewriting the present value of an annuity, equation (9.8) in functional notation gives equation (9.13).

$$PV = Payment \times PVIFA(k, n) \tag{9.13}$$

The present value of all loan payments must equal the present value, the value in today's dollars, of the item being financed. Suppose one was purchasing a $350,000 house, putting $50,000 down, and financing $300,000; for 30 years at 6% interest. What would each payment be? The period interest rate is 0.5% (6% APR/12 payments per year) and the number of periods is 360 (30 years x 12 payments per year.) Inputting what we know into equation (9.13) gives

$$\$300,000 = Payment \times PVIFA(0.5\%, 360)$$

$300,000 is the amount being financed. We can look up PVIFA(0.5%, 360) in the Present Value Interest Factor for an Annuity table. Read down the left most column to find n=360 then read across to period interest of 0.5% to find 166.792.

$$\$300,000 = Payment \times 166.79161$$

$$Payment = \$300,000 / 166.79161$$

$$= \$1,798.65$$

For periods and interest rates not in tables, use equation (9.6) to compute the Present Value Interest Factor for an Annuity. Make sure to adjust the discount rate by dividing the annual percentage rate by the number of payments per year, and adjust n by multiplying the number of periods per year times the number of years.

Loan Amortization Schedules

A loan amortization schedule analyzes principal and interest. Each loan payment must be separated into the interest portion and the principal portion. The principal portion is the amount that reduces the loan balance. Suppose interest is 6% per year on a 30 year, $300,000 loan. The period interest is 0.5% (6%/12 payments per year). Each payment is $1,798.65.

Find the interest on each payment by multiplying the period interest rate times the prior loan balance. Subtract the interest from the payment amount to find the amount of the payment which is used to reduce the principal balance. Subtract this amount from the prior month's principal balance. In the example in Table 9-1 Loan Amortization

Schedule, the interest on the first payment is $1,500 (0.5% x $300,000 loan balance. The first payment reduces the loan balance by $298.65 ($1,798.65 loan payment - $1,500 interest). Repeat these steps until the loan balance is reduced to zero.

Table 9-1 Loan Amortization Schedule

Payment Number	Payment Amount	Interest	Principal Payment	Principal Balance
				300,000.00
1	1,798.65	1,500.00	298.65	299,701.35
2	1,798.65	1,498.51	300.14	299,401.21
3	1,798.65	1,497.01	301.64	299,099.56
4	1,798.65	1,495.50	303.15	298,796.41
5	1,798.65	1,493.98	304.67	298,491.74
6	1,798.65	1,492.46	306.19	298,185.55
7	1,798.65	1,490.93	307.72	297,877.83
8	1,798.65	1,489.39	309.26	297,568.57
9	1,798.65	1,487.84	310.81	297,257.76
10	1,798.65	1,486.29	312.36	296,945.40

For a long term loan, very little of the early payments is applied to reduce the loan balance. For this reason, many pay additional principal each month to shorten the loan. For example, make payment number 1 of $1,798.65 plus the next month's principal payment of $300.14, and the next payment due would be payment number 3. This strategy saves the $1,498.51 of interest on payment number 2. Paying a payment plus the next month's principal payment will cut the loan length in half and save hundreds of thousands of dollars of interest.

Bonds

Bond Valuation

Corporations issue bonds for long term financing and to avoid the uncertainty of dealing with banks. Corporate bonds pay interest twice per year, but the face value of the bond is not paid until it matures. A bond's value is the present value of two payment streams; the present value of the periodic interest payments; and the present value of the face value of the bond. A bond's market value may be greater or less than the face value of the bond. Bond value can be computed using equation (9.14).

$$Vb= Payment \times PVIFA(k, n) + FV \times PVIF(k, n) \qquad (9.14)$$

Where Vb is the value of the bond, Payment is the semi-annual interest payment, PVIFA is the present value interest factor for an annuity, k is the period discount rate, n is the number of periods, which is the same as the number of payments, FV is the face value of the bond, and PVIF is the present value interest factor. The period discount rate k, is the yield on bonds of comparable risk divided by two periods per year.

Payments can be computed using equation (9.15).

Payment = FV x (coupon rate / 2 payments per year)   (9.15)

Suppose a $1 million ten year bond has a coupon rate of 5.2% interest per year, each interest payment would be

= $1,000,000 x (5.2% / 2)

= $26,000

Further, suppose bonds of comparable risk yield 6% per year. The period discount rate would be 3% (6% per year / 2 payments per year.) The number of periods would be 20 (10 years x 2 payments per year). Using equation (9.14) the bond value can be computed.

= $26,000 x PVIFA (3%, 20) + $1,000,000 x PVIF (3%, 20)

= $26,000 x 14.8775 + $1,000,000 x 0.55368

= $386,815 + $553,680

= $940,495

Bond Sinking Fund

Sometimes a company will set aside money each month so that when bonds come due, it will have cash to redeem them. This is called a sinking fund. Suppose a company issues a ten year, $1 million bond and sets up a sinking fund which will be invested at 4% per year and payments to the fund will be made monthly. The period interest rate will be 0.3333% (4% APR/12 payments per year) and the number of periods will be 120 (ten years x 12 payments per year). How much will each payment be?

FV= Payment x FVIFA(i, n)   (9.16)

Where FV is the face value of the bond, i is the period interest rate and n is the number of periods.

$1,000,000= Payment x FVIFA(0.3333%, 120)

Payment = $1,000,000 / 147.2495

= $6,791.19

Growth Rate

Investors often want to know how quickly a company's sales are growing or its earnings are growing. One could compute year over year growth rate, but companies have good years and bad, so by selecting different two year periods one could show good, bad or average growth. A better procedure is to look at the compound annual growth rate over several years.

The long term growth rate for sales, earnings or any other variable can be determined by modifying equation (9.1). Replace PV with the value in the base year, replace FV with the value in the ending year, and replace i with g; n is the number of years over which growth is measured. With a little algebra we get equation (9.17) which can be used to compute the compound annual growth rate of some variable.

$$g = ((\text{End Year Value} / \text{Base Year Value})^{(1/n)} - 1 \qquad (9.17)$$

Where g is growth rate, end year value is the value that something has grown to and the base year value is the starting point for growth, and n is the period over which growth is measured.

Suppose a company starts with sales of $6 million and ends with sales of $12 million over a three year period. What is its compound annual growth rate?

$$= [(\$12 \text{ million} / \$6 \text{ million})^{(1/3)}] - 1$$

$$= [2.0^{(1/3)}] - 1$$

$$= 1.2599 - 1$$

$$= 25.99\% \text{ per year}$$

Growth rates are always stated as a percentage. The growth rate in sales, spending, production, other variables can be estimated using this formula. If sales or other variables are declining, the rate of decline can also be estimated using this method.

Conclusion

Money loses value over time because of inflation and other factors. The time value of money provides a way to compare the value of money invested or received today to money to be spent or received in the future.

The future value interest factor estimates the amount of money one will have in the future if a single amount is invested at a given interest rate for a given period of time. The present value interest factor estimates the value in current dollars of an amount to be received in the future at a given discount rate. The future value interest factor of an annuity estimates how much one will have if one saves a regular amount each period for a number of years and that amount is invested at interest. The present value interest factor of an annuity estimates the value in current dollars of a series of regular payments to be received in the future at a given discount rate. The time value of money can also be used to compute loan payments, loan amortization schedules, bond value, bond sinking fund payments, and growth rates.

CHAPTER 10

Capital Budgeting

Introduction

Capital budgeting is about ranking large investments in plant, property, equipment, research and development projects, and in other companies. There is never enough money to invest in all the capital equipment, plant and so forth that a company may want, so some method must be found to rank investments. Investment decisions are also complicated by the fact that investments are made in current dollars and the return on those investments is harvested in future dollars over a period of years.

There are five basic methods of ranking investments (i) payback, (ii) discounted payback, (iii) net present value, (iv) internal rate of return, and (v) modified internal rate of return. Most sophisticated companies use several methods to rank projects.

Payback

Payback ranks projects based on how many years it takes to recover invested dollars. The process starts with an investment, which is called a cash outflow, and the cash inflows generated by the investment are subtracted one after the other until the next cash inflow exceeds the amount of the outflow. This is the number of years needed for payback. The amount not recovered by these years is called the residual. The residual is divided by the next year's inflow to find a fractional year.

Suppose a company invests $1,000,000 in a project, and it has cash inflows from the investment of $300,000, $400,000, and $500,000. What is the payback period?

Investment	$1,000,000
Less	
Year1 Inflow	$300,000
Year2 Inflow	$400,000
Residual	$300,000

Fraction of year $300,000 / $500,000 = .6

The payback for this project is 2.6 years. Short payback projects should be selected in preference to longer payback projects. The major advantage of this method is simplicity.

One drawback of this method is that it does not consider the time value of money. Dollars received in future years are worth less than the dollars used for the investment.

Discounted Payback

Discounted payback considers the time value of money and subtracts the present value of cash inflows from the investment cash outflow. To use this method, some discount rate must be estimated. Some argue the appropriate discount rate is the Weighted Average Cost of Capital (WACC). This is somewhat naïve because WACC implies the project is not making any more money than it is using. WACC does not take into account the fact that new increments of capital may cost more than currently used capital. Finally, WACC does not take into account the risk that actual cash inflows may be different than the estimates used in the capital budgeting process. A more sensible discount rate might be WACC plus some management determined increment like three to five percent.

Suppose a company makes an investment of $1,000,000 and has cash inflows of $300,000, $400,000, $500,000 and $600,000. If the Weighted Average Cost of Capital is 10% and the risk premium on projects is 5% the discount rate should be15%.

	Inflow x Discount		Discounted Cash Flow
Year1	$300,000 x PVIF(15%, 1) = $300,000 x	.86957	= $260,871
Year2	$400,000 x PVIF(15%, 2) = $400,000 x	.75614	= $302,456
Year3	$500,000 x PVIF(15%, 3) = $500,000 x	.65752	= $328,760
Year4	$600,000 x PVIF(15%, 4) = $600,000 x	.57175	= $343,050

Investment	$1,000,000	
Less		
Year1 Discounted Inflow	$260,871	
Year2 Discounted Inflow	$302,456	
Year3 Discounted Inflow	$328,760	
Residual	$107,913	
Fraction of Year	$107,913 / $343,050	= .31

The discounted payback for this project is 3.31 years. The shorter the payback the better. Short payback projects should be selected in preference to longer payback projects. The benefit of this method is that it is relatively simple. A drawback of both the payback and discounted payback methods is that they do not consider cash inflows in years after the payback period. Suppose projects A and B require investment of $1,000,000; project A cash inflows are $300,000, $400,000, and $500,000. Project B has cash inflows of $200,000, $300,000, $400,000, $500,000, and $600,000. The payback method would rank project A higher even though project B generates $800,000 more over its life than project A.

Net Present Value

Net present value (NPV) is the present value of all cash inflows less the present value of all cash outflows as shown by equation (10.1). Net present value represents the new wealth created by a project.

$$NPV = \Sigma \text{ Cash Inflow}_i \times PVIF(k, i) - \Sigma \text{ Cash Outflow}_j \times PVIF(k, j) \qquad (10.1)$$

Where the symbol "Σ" is the sum sign. Cash Inflow$_i$ is the cash inflow in year i, PVIF is the present value interest factor, k is the discount rate, i is the year of the cash inflow, Cash Outflow$_j$ is the cash outflow or investment in year j. This equation can be read as, "sum (add up) the present value of the cash inflows and subtract the present value of the cash outflows (investments). Investments made at the outset of a project are already in present dollars and need not be discounted.

Suppose a company has a project which requires a $1,000,000 investment; it will generate cash inflows of $300,000, $400,000, $500,000 and $600,000; and the company uses a 15% discount rate. What is the net present value of the project?

NPV   = $300,000 x PVIF(15%, 1) + $400,000 x PVIF(15%, 2)
          + $500,000 x PVIF(15%, 3) + $600,000 x PVIF(15%, 4)
          - $1,000,000

$$= \$300{,}000 \times 0.86957 + \$400{,}000 \times 0.75614 + \$600{,}000 \times 0.65752$$
$$+ \$600{,}000 \times 0.57175 - \$1{,}000{,}000$$

$$= \$260{,}871 + \$302{,}456 + \$328{,}760 + \$343{,}050 - \$1{,}000{,}000$$

$$= \$235{,}137$$

A present value of zero or less means the project should be rejected because it is destroying wealth.

Net present value is hailed by academics as the theoretically correct way to evaluate capital projects. However, it has a serious limitation. It doesn't consider the size of the investment. Suppose project A has a net present value of $20,000 and project B has a net present value of $10,000. Which should a company chose? On the surface it might seem Project A should be selected because it creates more wealth. Would it make any difference if you knew the cost of project A was $1,000,000 and the cost of project B was $30,000? One way to improve net present value as a project ranking method is to divide net present value by the amount of the investment to get the Investment Adjusted NPV as shown in equation (10.2).

Investment Adjusted NPV	= NPV / Investment	(10.2)
Investment Adjusted NPV-A	= $20,000 / $1,000,000	
	= 0.02	
Investment Adjusted NPV-B	= $10,000 / $30,000	
	= 0.33	

A higher Investment Adjusted NPV is better than a lower Investment Adjusted NPV. In the above example, a company might be able to complete 3 B projects at a cost of $90,000 and generate $30,000 of NPV as compared to Project A's $20,000 NPV on an investment of $1,000,000.

Internal Rate of Return

Internal Rate of Return (IRR) is the discount rate, k, that yields a net present value of zero. So IRR is the discount rate that makes the variable "test" equal to zero in equation (10.3).

$$\text{test} = \Sigma \text{ Cash Inflow}_i \times \text{PVIF}(k, i) - \Sigma \text{ Cash Outflow}_j \times \text{PVIF}(k, j) \qquad (10.3)$$

An advantage of IRR is that it can be directly compared to the return on other investments such as the return on a CD or the return on a stock.

The difficulty solving an equation like this is that the output, zero is known, but it is the input, k, that must be solved for. Oddly enough one can solve for IRR by making something out of nothing. Using judgment, select a k1 which is thought to be less than a project's IRR and a value k2 thought to be greater than a project's IRR to get outputs from equation (10.3) called test1 and test2 respectively. If the selection of k1 and k2 are appropriate, test1 will be greater than zero, and test2 will be less than zero. These data can then be input to equation (10.4) which can be solved for IRR.[1]

$$\frac{test2 - test1}{k2 - k1} = \frac{0 - test1}{IRR - k1} \qquad (10.4)$$

Suppose a project has a cash outflow (investment) of $1,000,000 and cash inflows of $300,000, $400,000, $500,000 and $600,000. What is its internal rate of return?

Since there is no point in funding a project that returns less than the discount rate used to compute NPV, let k1 be 15%. This represents the lowest estimate of the project's IRR. We don't know what the upper limit of IRR is, so we pick something substantially larger than k1. Let k2 equal 30%.

test1 = $300,000 x PVIF(15%, 1) + $400,000 x PVIF(15%, 2)
+ $500,000 x PVIF(15%, 3) + $600,000 x PVIF(15%, 4)
- $1,000,000
= $260,871 + $302,456 + $328,760 + $343,050 - $1,000,000
= $235,137

test2 = $300,000 x PVIF(30%, 1) + $400,000 x PVIF(30%, 2)
+ $500,000 x PVIF(30%, 3) + $600,000 x PVIF(30%, 4)
- $1,000,000
= $230,769 + $236,688 + $227,585 + $210,078 - $1,000,000
= -$94,880

Applying these data to equation (10.4)

$$\frac{-\$94,880 - \$235,137}{30\% - 15\%} = \frac{0 - \$235,137}{IRR - 15\%}$$

Multiplying both sides by -1 gives

$$\frac{\$330,017}{15\%} = \frac{\$235,167}{(IRR - 15\%)}$$

1 Consider a graph where the output of the right side of equation (10.3) is plotted on the y-axis and discount rates are plotted along the x-axis. If values starting at k = 0 are input to (10.3) and incremented by 0.01%, one could plot a line which would curve down and to the right crossing the x-axis. The k value that causes the line to cross the x-axis is the IRR. One can draw two lines. One from the coordinates test1, k1 to test2, k2 and one from coordinates test1, k1 to 0, IRR. The slopes of these lines are almost the same. Setting the slopes of these two lines equal to one another gives equation (10.4). Every thing is known in this equation except IRR, so with a little algebra, IRR can be estimated.

Cross multiplying the denominators and dividing both sides by \$330,047 gives

IRR – 15%	= (\$235,137 / \$330,017) x 15%
IRR	= 15% + 10.69%
	= 25.69%

Recall this is an estimate of IRR. The estimate can be refined by selecting a k1 and k2 closer to the real IRR. If a more precise estimate is needed, one can select a k1 2% less than the initial IRR estimate and a k2 which is 2% higher than the initial IRR estimate. A second order estimate is usually accurate to within a few tenths of a percent which is more than sufficient for capital budgeting. These calculations can be set up as a spreadsheet which makes evaluation of a series of projects quick and efficient.

Modified Internal Rate of Return

When investments are made in a project in more than one year, IRR can have multiple values one of which is correct and the others are incorrect. Two examples come to mind. One might construct a nuclear power plant for \$8 billion, then, 40 years later, it might cost another \$2 billion to decommission the plant and clean up the site. One might spend \$10 million to buy a mountain and another \$4 million to scrape off the overburden for an open pit coal mine. When the mine is closed 20 years later, the land must be restored, and that might take another \$5 million.

The year when a project ends is called the terminal year. The modified internal rate of return computes the future value of all cash inflows and outflows to the terminal year, then discounts the result back to the present. The discount rate which makes all calculations sum to zero is the modified internal rate of return (MIRR).

There is considerable controversy in applying this methodology. Question one is whether the interest rate used to compute the future value to the terminal date should be the same as the discount rate used to compute the present value. The argument against using the same rate is that there is no guarantee that cash inflows can be re-invested at the same rate generated by the project. The counter argument is that there is no guarantee what rate cash flows will be invested at under any circumstances and a project should not be burdened by doubt as to what management will do with the proceeds.

Assume for a moment that the interest rate used to compute future value and the discount rate used to compute present value are the same. MIRR is the rate which will make the variable "test" in equation (10.5) equal to zero.

$$\text{test} = \text{PVIF}(k, n) \times [\Sigma \text{ Cash Inflow}_i \times \text{FVIF}(k, t - i) - \Sigma \text{ Cash Outflow}_j \times \text{FVIF}(k, t - j)] \qquad (10.5)$$

The variable "test" is the value which will be driven to zero when the correct k is found. Using the MIRR method k is the discount rate as well as the interest rate used to compute future value. The terminal year of the project is t. The sum of the future value of cash inflows is computed at k interest for the period t minus year i. For cash outflows the period is t − j where j is the period of the cash outflow.

MIRR can be estimated by selecting a k1 which provides a positive value for test in equation (10.5) and a k2 which provides a negative value for test, call these test values test1 and test2 respectively. Replace IRR in equation (10.4) with MIRR to get equation (10.6). Since all variables are known except MIRR, algebra is sufficient to solve the problem.

$$\frac{test2 - test1}{k2 - k1} = \frac{0 - test1}{MIRR - k1} \qquad (10.6)$$

Suppose a project has a cash outflow (investment) of $1,000,000 and cash inflows are $300,000, $400,000, $500,000 and $600,000. What is its modified internal rate of return? Let k1 be 15% and k2 be 30%. Year 4 is the terminal year of the project.

```
test1 = PVIF(15%, 4) x [$300,000 x FVIF(15%, (4 -1)) +$400,000 x FVIF(15%, (4 -2))
            + $500,000 x FVIF(15%, 4 -3) + $600,000 X FVIF(15%, (4 -4))
                $1,000,000 X FVIF (15%, (4 – 0))]
      = 0.57175 X [$300,000 x 1.52088 + $400,000 x 1.3225
            + $500,000 x 1.15 + $600,000 - $1,000,000 x 1.74901]
      = 0.57175 x [$456,264 + $529,000 + $575,000 + $600,000 - $1,749,010]
      = 0.57175 x $411,254
      = $235,134
```

```
test2 = PVIF(30%, 4) x [$300,000 x FVIF(30%, (4 -1)) +$400,000 x FVIF(30%, (4 -2))
            + $500,000 x FVIF(30%, (4 -3)) + $600,000 X FVIF(30%, (4 -4))
                $1,000,000 X FVIF(30%, (4 – 0))]
      = .35013 x [$659,100 + $676,000 + $650,000 + $600,000 - $2,856,100]
      = .35013 x [-$271,000]
      = -$94,885
```

Applying equation (10.6)

$$\frac{-\$94,885 - \$235,134}{30\% - 15\%} = \frac{0 - \$235,134}{MIRR - 15\%}$$

$$\frac{-\$330,019}{15\%} = \frac{-\$235,134}{(MIRR - 15\%)}$$

Multiplying both sides by -1; dividing both sides by $330,019 and multiplying both sides by (MIRR − 15%) gives,

MIRR + 15%= ($235,134/330,019) x 15%

MIRR = .7125 x 15% + 15%

= 25.69%

There is no reason that IRR and MIRR should be exactly the same. Never the less, experience shows that they are usually within a few percentage points of each other.

Precision of IRR and MIRR

The precision of IRR and MIRR estimates can be evaluated by plugging them into equations (10.3 and (10.5) respectively. If the estimate is perfect, the variable "test" will be equal to zero. A rough estimate of the quality of the solution can be gauged by dividing the absolute value computed for "test" by the investment. The estimate of IRR, above was 25.69%. Using that as k in equation (10.3) gives,

test = $300,000 x PVIF(25.69%, 1) + $400,000 x PVIF(25.69%, 2)
           + $500,000 x PVIF(25.69%, 3) + $600,000 x PVIF(25.69%, 4)
                - $1,000,000

Since there are no tables for the discount rate of 25.69% one must use the present value interest factor formula from Chapter 9.

test = $300,000 x (1 / (1.2569)) + $400,000 x (1 / (1.2569)^2)
              + $500,000 x (1 / (1.2569)^3) + $600,000 x (1 / (1.2569)^4)
                 - $1,000,000
     = $300,000 x .79561 + $400,000 x .63299
           + $500,000 x .50361 + $600,000 x .40068
              - $1,000,000
     = $238,683 + $253,196 + $251,805 + $240,408 - $1,000,000
     =   -$15,909

An estimate of precision can be made using equation (10.7). The vertical bars surrounding the equation indicate one should use the absolute value of this ratio.

Precision= |test / Investment| (10.7)

   = $15,909 / $1,000,000

   = 1.59%

Precision may be increased by selecting K1 and K2 closer to the true value of IRR or MIRR as the case may be. One could select a new k1 as the first estimate of IRR -2% and select a new k2 which is the first estimate of IRR +2%. In the alternative one could select closer k1 and k2 values from Present Value Interest Factor tables.

Let k1 equal 24% and recompute IRR.

$$
\begin{aligned}
\text{test1} &= \$300,000 \times PVIF(24\%, 1), + \$400,000 \times PVIF(24\%, 2) \\
&\quad + \$500,000 \times PVIF(24\%, 3) + \$600,000 \times PVIF(24\%, 4) \\
&\quad - \$1,000,000 \\
&= \$241,935 + \$260,144 + \$262,245 + \$253,782 - \$1,000,000 \\
&= \$18,106
\end{aligned}
$$

We already have test2, so we can plug this data into equation (10.4).

$$
\frac{-\$94,880 - \$18,106}{30\% - 24\%} = \frac{0 - \$18,106}{IRR - 24\%}
$$

$$
\frac{\$112,986}{6\%} = \frac{\$18,106}{(IRR-24\%)}
$$

$$
IRR = (\$18,106/\$112,986) \times 6\% + 24\%
$$

$$
= 24.96\%
$$

To test this for precision, recompute test.

$$
\begin{aligned}
\text{test} &= \$300,000 \times PVIF(24.96\%, 1) + \$400,000 \times PVIF(24.96\%, 2) \\
&\quad + \$500,000 \times PVIF(24.96\%, 3) + \$600,000 \times PVIF(24.96\%, 4) \\
&\quad - \$1,000,000 \\
&= \$240,077 + \$256,164 + \$256,246 + \$246,075 - \$1,000,000 \\
&= \$1,438
\end{aligned}
$$

$$
\begin{aligned}
\text{Precision} &= |\ \$1,438 / \$1,000,000\ | \\
&= 0.14\%
\end{aligned}
$$

The difference between the first and second estimates was only 0.73% (25.69% -24.96%) which is probably close enough to rank capital budgeting projects because estimates of cash inflows and outflows are usually much less precise than this.

While this methodology may seem computationally intense, once set up on a spreadsheet, estimation of IRR and MIRR to any given level of precision becomes trivial.

Estimating Cash Flow

Cash inflows and outflows used in capital budgeting analyses are net cash inflows and outflows. Projects usually have three sets of cash flows (i) initial cash outflows to set up the project, (ii) cash inflows from operations and (iii) cash inflows from terminating the project.

Cash outflows include the initial investment for plant, property and equipment, engineering studies, costs to install and test machinery and working capital for inventory and accounts receivables.

Cash flow from operations is different from operating profit. Cash flow from operations includes profits plus depreciation, amortization and depletion, and adjustments to working capital if inventory or accounts receivable are growing or shrinking.

Terminal cash flow includes cash generated from operations in the terminal year, plus recovery of working capital as inventory is sold off and accounts receivable are collected and cash inflows from sale of plant, property and equipment.

Optimum Capital Budget

Sophisticated companies use all five techniques to rank projects. Projects that rank high under all techniques are funded first, and then lower ranking projects are funded if funds are available.

Companies use the least cost funds first, then more and more expensive sources of capital. The cheapest funds for most companies are retained earnings and bank loans. Suppose a bank wants a company to maintain a debt equity ratio of 2:1, then each dollar of new retained earnings (undistributed profits) will enable a company to borrow two dollars. The next most expensive money might be second mortgages on real estate, commercial credit companies, and so forth. It is beyond the scope of this book to provide a complete list of funding sources and their relative cost.[2] As a company seeks more and more funds, the Marginal Cost of Capital (MCC) will rise. One can generate a curve, or more realistically a set of steps that plot the Marginal Cost of Capital where cost is on the Y-axis and the incremental amount of funds is on the X-axis. This will give rise to a curve that rises as it moves to the right. See Table 10.2 for Optimal Capital Budget.

If projects are ranked from those with the highest internal rate of return to the lowest rate of internal return, a curve can be generated which starts high on the left and declines as it moves to the right. This is sometimes called an Investment Opportunities Schedule (IOS). The internal rate of return is plotted on the Y-axis and amount required by each project plotted on the X-axis.

2 See *Raising Capital by David E. Vance. Springer Science & Business Media. New York. 2005.*

Table 10-2: Optimum Capital Budget

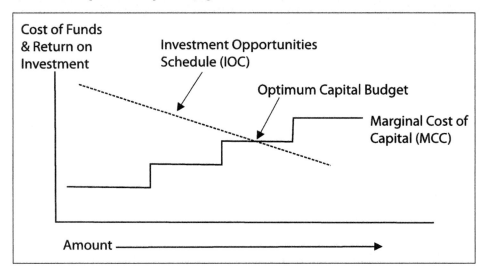

In theory, the optimum capital budget is where the IOC and MCC curves cross. If any part of a project would be funded by capital that costs more than its internal rate of return, that project is rejected. Since there is some level of uncertainty in forecasting cash flows, the prudent thing would be to demand that every project funded exceed its cost of funds by some amount, for example 5%. The exact percent selected is a matter for management judgment.

Conclusion

Large, long term projects are difficult to evaluate because start up costs are paid in current dollars and the benefits accrue over a number of years and will be received in future dollars which are less valuable than the dollars which went into the initial investment. Methods for evaluating large, long term projects are called capital budgeting.

There are five primary methods of evaluating capital projects (i) payback – which is the number of years it takes to recover an initial investment, (ii) discounted payback – which is the number of years it takes to recover an initial investment in present dollars, (iii) net present value – which is the sum of the present value of all the cash inflows less the sum of the present value of all cash outflows, (iv) internal rate of return which is the discount rate which will drive net present value to zero, and (v) modified internal rate of return which is very complex but used when there are multiple years of cash outflows..

The decision rule for payback and discounted payback is to rank projects with the shortest payback or discounted payback highest. The decision rule for net present value is to reject projects where the net present value is zero or less. Ranking net present value projects is difficult, but it helps to divide net present value by the investment. Under this method, the higher the investment adjusted net present value the better. The higher the internal rate of return or modified internal rate of return, the better.

Sophisticated companies use multiple methods to rank projects. Projects that rank highest using every method are funded first. Those at the bottom of every ranking are probably not funded. Those in the middle require additional management scrutiny.

As a company seeks more capital, the incremental cost of capital will rise. The incremental cost of capital can be plotted as an upward sloping line, or upward sloping set of steps. Projects ranked from the highest internal rate of return to the lowest can be plotted as a line that slopes downward and to the right. In theory the optimum capital budget is the one where these two curves intersect. However, since there is usually some uncertainty in cash flow projections, a prudent manager might stop funding projects when the excess of project return over the cost of capital reaches some minimum value like 5%. The exact percent is a matter of management judgment.

CHAPTER 11

Investment Banking

Introduction

Investment banking involves many services including buying, selling and valuing companies. It also involves advising companies on mergers and acquisitions and how to maximize value. This chapter discusses ratios investment bankers might use. A comprehensive discussion of investment banking strategies is beyond the scope of this book.

Market Capitalization

Market Capitalization, often shortened to Market Cap, is the total number of shares outstanding times the market price of those shares. The number of shares outstanding can be found in the income statement, after net income. If a company is large and publicly traded its share price can be found in the Wall Street Journal. The share price of large and small publicly traded firms can be found at finance.yahoo.com. The formula for Market Cap is given by equation (11.1).

Market Cap= Outstanding Shares x Market Price   (11.1)

Suppose a company has ten million shares outstanding and its market price is $16 per share. What is the Market Cap of the company?

Market Cap = 10 million x $16

          = $160 million

Market Cap is always quoted in dollars. Market Cap has no meaning if a company is not publicly traded. Where stocks are thinly traded, the last recorded share price might not be a good indicator of value. Thinly traded stocks are those where a few hundred shares a day or less are traded. For some small companies there may be week or months between trades.

Book Value

The book value of a company is the value of its assets less the value of its liabilities. Assets less Liabilities is Equity. Book Value is generally thought to represent a company's minimum value. It does not consider appreciation of assets held for use in the business. Nor does it consider the income producing potential of the business. Some suggest that when market cap is less than book value, that represents a buying opportunity.

Estimating Company Value

Market Capitalization and Book Value are simple mechanical ways to value a company, but there are many other ways. Ultimately a company's value at a point in time is what someone is willing and able to pay for it. Company valuation fluctuates all the time. As such, the best one can do between sales is to estimate its value.

Company value may be estimated by analyzing what was paid for similar companies. Since no two companies are exactly the same size, some common denominator must be used to adjust for size. This gives rise to a series of multiplier methods.

Valuation Using the EBITDA Multiplier

The EBITDA Multiplier method determines what the market is willing to pay for a dollar of EBITDA in companies similar to the one being valued. EBITDA is earnings before interest, taxes, depreciation and amortization. It is a rough estimate of cash flow from operations. The formula for the EBITDA Multiplier is given by equation (11.2).

$$\text{EBITDA Multiplier} \quad = \quad \sum_{1}^{n} \text{Market Cap}_i / \sum_{1}^{n} \text{EBITDA}_i \qquad (11.2)$$

Where n is the number of companies that are used to create the EBITDA Multiplier, Market Cap$_i$ is the market cap of the ith company used as the basis of comparison and EBITDA$_i$ is the EBITDA of the ith company in the comparison. Equation (11.2) would be read, sum all the Market Cap's from company 1 to company n; then divide that by the sum of the EBITDA's from company 1 to company n.

Suppose one were trying to value a company which makes solar cells. The first step is to compile information on other companies the make solar cells as shown in Table 11-1 Solar Cell Manufacturers. Table 11-1 already contains totals for Market Cap and EBITDA. Applying them to equation (11.2) yields,

= 1,340.0 / 297.0

= 4.51

Table 11-1 Solar Cell Manufacturers

All numbers except share price are in millions

Company	Sales	EBITDA	Net Income	Out-standing Shares	Price	Market Cap
Alpha Industries	300.0	95.0	55.0	100.0	4.50	450.0
Beta Electronics	200.0	65.0	42.0	200.0	1.10	220.0
Gamma Materials	52.0	32.0	100.0	2.00	200.0	150.0
Delta Devices	120.0	40.0	22.0	20.0	12.00	240.0
Epsilon Electronics	90.0	25.0	20.0	10.0	15.00	150.0
Zeta Solar	60.0	20.0	16.0	20.0	4.00	80.0
Totals	920.0	297.0	187.0			1,340.0

The EBITDA Multiplier is always dimensionless. To estimate the value of a company, multiply its EBITDA times the industry EBITDA Multiplier as shown in equation (11.3).

Estimated Value= Target Company EBITDA x EBITDA Multiplier   (11.3)

The Target Company is the one being valued. Suppose the target company has an EBITDA of $5.0 million. Estimate its value using the EBITDA Multiplier Method.

= $5.0 million x 4.51

= $22.6 million

The EBITDA Multiplier cannot be used when a company has an EBITDA which is close to zero or negative. Likewise the companies selected to compute the EBITDA Multiplier must have an EBITDA which is positive and not close to zero.

Valuation Using the Sales Multiplier

The Sales Multiplier method uses the relationship between market cap and sales to value companies. Sometimes this method is called the Revenue Multiplier Method. The formula for the Sales Multiplier is given in equation (11.4).

$$\text{Sales Multiplier} = \sum_{1}^{n} \text{Market Cap}_i / \sum_{1}^{n} \text{Sales}_i \qquad (11.4)$$

Where Market Cap$_i$ is the market cap of the ith company, Sales$_i$ is the Sales of the ith company, and n is the number of companies used to compute the multiplier. Using data from Table 11-1 Solar Cell Manufacturers

$$= 1,340.0 / 920.0$$
$$= 1.46$$

To estimate a target company's value using the Sales Multiplier method, multiply its sales times the Sales Multiplier as shown in equation (11.5).

$$\text{Estimated Value} = \text{Target Company Sales} \times \text{Sales Multiplier} \qquad (11.5)$$

Suppose the target company has sales of $15.0 million. Estimate its value using the Sales Multiplier method.

$$= \$15.0 \text{ million} \times 1.46$$
$$= \$21.9 \text{ million}$$

There is no reason why estimates of company value should be the same using different methods. Nevertheless, multiple estimates provide a consensus as to a company's real value.

Valuation Using the Net Income Multiplier

The Net Income Multiplier method uses the relationship between market cap and net income to value a company. The formula for the Net Income Multiplier is given in equation (11.6).

$$\text{Net Income Multiplier} = \sum_{1}^{n} \text{Market Cap}_i / \sum_{1}^{n} \text{Net Income}_i \qquad (11.6)$$

Where Market Cap$_i$ is the market cap of the ith company and Net Income$_i$ is the Net Income of the ith company and n is the number of companies used to compute the multiplier. Using data from Table 11-1 Solar Cell Manufacturers

$$= 1340.0 / 187.0$$
$$= 7.17$$

The Net Income Multiplier cannot be used when a company has a Net Income which is close to zero or negative. Likewise the companies selected to compute the Net Income Multiplier must have a Net Income which is positive and not close to zero.

To estimate a target company's value using the Net Income Multiplier method, multiply its Net Income times the Net Income Multiplier as shown in equation (11.7).

Estimated Value= Target Company Net Income x Net Income Multiplier (11.7)

Suppose the target company has Net Income of $3.0 million. Estimate its value using the Net Income Multiplier method.

= $3.0 million x 7.17

= $21.5 million

The net income multiplier method has been criticized because income from operations is masked by a company's financing and tax strategy. The argument is that the EBITDA multiplier method provides a better estimate of value because it is more directly tied to operating performance. The counter argument is that one should value a company based on the net income available to shareholders rather than its income producing potential.

Value per Customer

Where companies have large numbers of homogeneous (similar) customers, value per customer can provide a common denominator for valuation. The industry average value per customer can be determined using equation (11.8).

$$\text{Industry Value per Customer} = \sum_{1}^{n} \text{Market Cap}_i / \sum_{1}^{n} \text{Customers}_i \qquad (11.8)$$

Suppose Table 11-2 Electric Companies is an analysis of integrated electric power generation and distribution companies. Estimate the Value per Customer.

Table 11-2 Electric Companies

	Customers	Revenue	Outstanding Shares	Share Price	Market Cap
B is billions of dollars and M is millions of dollars					
Wisconsin Electric	1,200,000	$2.52B	88.0M	$20.00	$1.76B
Public Service Electric	3,900,000	$8.19B	126.0M	$65.00	$8.19B
Maine Electric	500,000	$0.85B	40.0M	$21.25	$0.85B
North Dakota Electric	600,000	$1.08B	72.0M	$15.00	$1.08B
South Dakota Electric	700,000	$1.19B	91.5M	$13.00	$1.90B
	6,900,000	$13.83B			$13.78B

= $13,780,000,000 / 6,900,000

= $1,997 per customer

131

Once the industry average value per customer is known, target company value can be estimated using equation (11.9).

Estimated Value= Target Company Customers x Value per Customer   (11.9)

Suppose the electric company being valued has 800,000 customers. Estimate its value.

= 800,0000 x $1,997 per customer

= $1,579,600,000 or $1.58 billion.

The value per customer method can be used for electric, cable, phone, water, gas and other companies that have a large number of homogeneous (similar) customers.

Debt Adjusted Company Valuation

When a company is purchased, the purchaser assumes responsibility for the company's debt. How does a company's debt affect its value?

Consider companies A & B with the following characteristics:

	A	A
Revenue	$50M	$50M
EBITDA	$10M	$10M
Net Income	$4M	$4M
Debt	$10M	$30M

The Revenue, EBITDA and Net Income multiplier method values would be the same for companies A and B, but would you pay the same? The EBITDA, Revenue and Net Income multipliers used to estimate company value assume companies have an average amount of debt. The assumption of an average debt masks a lot of detail.

Stock price adjusts somewhat for a company's debt, since market cap is share price times the number of shares outstanding. No public company is debt free so the market will never directly tell us the value of a debt free company.

If we computed the Revenue Multiplier (Market Value/Revenue) EBITDA Multiplier (Market Value/EBITDA) and Net Income Multiplier (Market Value/Net Income) for each company in an industry, there will be some range of variation for each of these ratios. Part of the difference in these ratios would be attributable to differences in debt level.

Suppose companies A & B were publicly traded with market capitalizations of $40M and $20M respectively. The revenue multipliers for A & B would be .8 ($40M/$50M) and .4 ($20M/$50M) respectively. The industry revenue multiplier would be .6 (($40M +$20M)/ ($50M +$50M)).

Assume the Total Value (TV) is the value of a company if it were debt free. All of its value would be allocated to the shareholders (owners.) For publicly traded companies the owner's value is the market value. If we assume that the every dollar of debt reduces a dollar of value allocated to shareholders, the Total Value (TV) of a company can be written as shown in equation (11.12):

$$TV = Market\ Value + Debt \qquad (11.12)$$

We can use total value to generate a new set of multipliers for Total Value Revenue Multiplier, equation (11.13), Total Value EBITDA Multiplier (11.14) and Total Value Net Income Multiplier (11.15) that should, theoretically, be more accurate than the commonly used multipliers.

$$TV\ Revenue\ Multiplier = \Sigma\,TV\ /\ \Sigma\ Revenue \qquad (11.13)$$

$$TV\ EBITDA\ Multiplier = \Sigma TV\ /\ \Sigma\ EBITDA \qquad (11.14)$$

$$TV\ Net\ Income\ Multiplier = S\ TV\ /\ S\ Net\ Income \qquad (11.15)$$

Consider the following Total Value (TV) Analysis where companies A and B represent the total industry.

	A	B	INDUSTRY
Market Value	$40M	$20M	$60M
Debt	$10M	$30M	$40M
Total Value (TV)	$50M	$50M	$100M
Revenue	$50M	$50M	$100M
TV Revenue Multiplier			1.0
EBITDA	$10M	$10M	$20M
TV EBITDA Multiplier			5.0
Net Income	$4M	$4M	$8M
TV Net Income Multiplier			12.5

After the total value is calculated, the debt load of each individual target company can be subtracted to compute a more refined estimate of company value. For example suppose we were valuing companies C & D with revenues of $20M and $25M and debt of $5M and $12M.

	C	D
Revenue	$20M	$25M
x TV Revenue Multiplier	x 1.0	x 1.0
TV	$20M	$25M
Less Debt	-5M	-12M
Debt Adjusted Revenue Multiplier Value	$15M	$13M

Compare this to the company valuations using the Revenue Multiplier unadjusted for debt assuming companies A and B represent the industry.

	C	D
Revenue	$20M	$25M
x Revenue Multiplier	x 0.6	x 0.6
Revenue Multiplier Method Value	$12M	$15M

In this example, the debt adjusted value of company C is $3M more than using multipliers based on average debt load. The debt adjusted value of company D is $2M less than using multipliers based on average debt load.

Adjustment for debt load can be generalized across all valuation methods that use market cap. For example, to generate debt adjusted multipliers, expand Table 11-1 by adding two columns; one for debt and one for debt plus market cap which is what the company would theoretically be worth if it was debt free. This last column would be its Total Value.

The sum of Total Value (TV) would replace the sum of Market Cap in equations (11.2), (11.4) and (11.6). These multipliers would be applied using equations (11.16), (11.17) and (11.18).

$$\text{Debt Adjusted EBITDA} = \text{TV EBITDA Multiplier} \times \text{EBITDA} - \text{Debt} \qquad (11.16)$$

$$\text{Debt Adjusted Revenue} = \text{TV Revenue Multiplier} \times \text{Revenue} - \text{Debt} \qquad (11.17)$$

$$\text{Debt Adjusted Net Income} = \text{TV Net Income Multiplier} \times \text{Net Income} - \text{Debt} \quad (11.18)$$

Where TV Multipliers are the debt adjusted industry multipliers and EBITDA, Revenue, Net Income and Debt are for the company being valued.

Revenue per Customer

Revenue per customer can be estimated using comparative analysis. Realistically, one will know the revenue of the company being valued, so why estimate it? The answer is that the company being valued may be underperforming its peers. This method is designed to estimate what its revenue should be, if it were exploiting all the revenue opportunities available to it. Revenue per customer can be estimated using equation (11.19).

$$\text{Revenue per Customer} = \sum_1^n \text{Revenue}_i / \sum_1^n \text{Customers}_i \qquad (11.19)$$

Using the data from Table 11-2 Electric Companies, an estimate can be made as to the revenue each customer can generate.

$$= \$13,830,000,000 / 6,900,000$$
$$= \$2,004 \text{ per customer}$$

Equation (11.20) can be used to estimate the revenue a company should have.

$$\text{Company Revenue} = \text{Revenue per Customer} \times \text{Customers} \qquad (11.20)$$

$$= \$2,004 \times 800,000$$
$$= \$1,603,200,000 \text{ or } \$1.60B$$

Suppose the Sales Multiplier for this industry is 0.996; the company's actual revenue is \$1.300B and the company could potentially generate \$1.60B if it were managed well enough to be average. How much additional value could be generated? Adapt equation (11.5) to get equation (11.21).

$$\text{Additional Value} = \text{Potential Sales} \times \text{Sales Multiplier} - \text{Current Sales} \times \text{Sales Multiplier} \qquad (11.21)$$

$$= \$1.60B \times .996 - \$1.300B \times .996$$
$$= \$0.299B \text{ or } \$299 \text{ million}$$

An investment bank might use the potential additional value to inform the upper limit on the premium it might pay for an acquisition, and it might also use this computation to estimate the value that could be harvested by acquiring, restructuring and selling a company.

Discounted Cash Flow (DCF)

Discounted Cash Flow (DCF) or more properly the Discounted Free Cash Flow is the most "theoretically correct" method of valuing a company. It sums the present value of discounted free cash flow for a company over a number of years to estimate company value as shown in equation (11.22).

$$\text{DCF Value} = \sum_{1}^{n} \text{Free Cash Flow}_i \times \text{PVIF (k, i)} \qquad (11.22)$$

Where Free Cash Flow$_i$ is the free cash flow generated in year i, PVIF is the Present Value Interest Factor, k is the discount rate, and i is the year of the cash inflow.

Table 11-3 Discounted Cash Flow Valuation provides an example of how this method is applied. The example uses a discount rate of 18% per year.

Table 11-3: Discounted Cash Flow Valuation

YEAR	FREE CASH FLOW	PVIF	DISCOUNTED CASH FLOW	YEAR	FREE CASH FLOW	PVIF	DISCOUNTED CASH FLOW
1	20.0	0.84746	16.9	6	30.0	0.37043	11.1
2	22.0	0.71818	15.8	7	32.0	0.31393	10.0
3	24.0	0.60863	14.6	8	34.0	0.26604	9.0
4	26.0	0.51579	13.4	9	36.0	0.22546	8.1
5	28.0	0.43711	12.2	10	38.0	0.19121	7.3

Company Value is the Sum of the Discounted Cash Flows: 118.4

The DCF method is fraught with practical problems. For example, it requires forecasting sales, expenses and other adjustments to cash far into the future. Selection of the discount rate is highly subjective and there is a question as to how many years of future cash flow should be included in the estimate.

Weighted Average Value

When a company is valued using multiple methods, one might use a weighted average to generate a single estimate to use in negotiations. Some valuation methods are favored by analysts more than others. For example, the EBITDA Multiplier Method is based on an estimate of cash flow and many analysts believe it is a more valid measure of a company's value than the Sales Multiplier Method, Net Income Multiplier Method or other valuation methods. As a result, they may choose to double or triple weight EBITDA in the weighted average estimate of value. The formula for the Weighted Average Value is given by equation (11.23).

$$\text{Weighted Average Value} \quad = \quad \sum_{1}^{n} W_i \times \text{Value}_i / \sum_{1}^{n} W_i \qquad (11.23)$$

Where n is the number of value estimates, W_i is the weight given to each estimate and Value_i is each estimated value.

Suppose a target company was valued at $21.5 million using the Net Income Multiplier Method; $21.9 million using the Sales Multiplier Method and $22.6 million using the EBITDA Multiplier Method. Further, suppose the EBITDA Multiplier Method were given twice the weight of the other estimates. Estimate the Weighted Average Value.

$$= \quad \frac{1 \times \$21.5 \text{ million} + 1 \times \$21.9 \text{ million} + 2 \times \$22.6 \text{ million}}{1 + 1 + 2}$$

= $88.6 million / 4

= $22.2 million

Adjustment of Accounting Data

Sales, EBITDA and Net Income of comparable companies and the target company may include one-time events that temporarily distort their value, more sophisticated analyses locate and adjust for these events. Where a private company is being valued, adjustments often have to be made for excess owner compensation.

Private Company Discount

Shares of a publicly traded company can be resold to anyone. Shares of a privately held company are restricted and generally cannot be resold. This restriction, imposed by the Securities Act of 1933, makes shares of a privately held company illiquid (hard to convert to cash). Illiquidity reduces the value of a privately held company by 25% to 30% as compared to a similar publicly traded company as shown in equation (11.24). Valuations estimated using the Revenue Multiplier, EBITDA Multiplier, Net Income Multiplier and Market Cap per Customer assume a company is publicly traded.

Private Company Value = Value Assuming Publicly Traded x (1- Discount)   (11.24)

Suppose a company would be worth $20 million as a publicly traded company, but it is privately held and the Discount for privately held companies in its industry is 25%. What is the value of the company as a privately held entity?

= $20 million x (1 – 25%)

= $20 million x 75%

= $15 million

A privately held company can become a publicly traded company by registering its shares with the Securities and Exchange Commission. Registration is complex and expensive and as such is only practical for companies with more than $100 million in sales.

Initial Public Offering Price

The first time a company sells stock to the public it is called an Initial Public Offering (IPO). Usually an investment bank is hired to manage the process of registering a company's shares with the SEC, buying any new shares the company issues and reselling them to institutional investors. The day before the IPO, the investment bank will agree with the company on the target price per share. Investment banks have a strong incentive to set the stock price low because that makes it easier to resell new shares. In addition, investment banks get options to buy additional shares at the offering price. The options become more valuable if the offering price is low. On the other hand, the company selling its stock should want to set the offering price as high as it can and still enable the investment banker to sell all the shares. Since there is an inherent conflict of interest in setting stock price, a company going public should independently estimate IPO share price.

The company value (CV) must be spread over old shareholders (OS) plus new shares (NS) as shown in equation (11.25).

$$\text{Target Price} = \frac{CV}{OS + NS} \qquad (11.25)$$

The amount raised by issuing new shares (Amt) must equal the Target Price times the number of new shares (NS) as shown in equation (11.26). This equation can be re-written as equation (11.27).

Amt   = Target Price x NS   (11.26)

Target Price = Amt / NS   (11.27)

We now have two equations (11.25) and (11.27) which both equal the Target Price per share. Setting these equations equal to each other gives equation (11.28)

$$\text{Amt} / NS = \frac{CV}{(OS + NS)} \tag{11.28}$$

Multiplying both sides by (OS + NS), then multiplying both sides by NS gives equation (11.29).

$$\text{Amt} \times (OS + NS) = CV \times NS \tag{11.29}$$

Solving for NS gives the equation (11.30).

$$NS = \frac{\text{Amt} * OS}{(CV - \text{Amt})} \tag{11.30}$$

Suppose a company is valued at \$10 million; wants to raise \$2 million in new capital and has 1.2 million shares outstanding. How many new shares should it issue? What should be the target price?

$$= \frac{\$2M * 1.2M}{(\$10M - \$2M)}$$

$$= \frac{\$2.4\,M}{\$8M}$$

= 0.3 M shares

Target Price = Amt / NS

= \$2M / 0.3M

= \$6.67 per share

A more complicated and controversial version of this analysis assumes that every dollar of capital raised increases the company's value by one dollar. This could be true if every dollar raised went to reduce debt. In that case equation (11.25) would be modified to become equation (11.31) and equation (11.30) would become equation (11.32)

$$\text{Target Price} = \frac{CV + \text{Amt}}{OS + NS} \tag{11.31}$$

$$NS = \frac{\text{Amt} \times OS}{CV} \tag{11.32}$$

Suppose a company is valued at \$10 million; wants to raise \$2 million in new capital and has 1.2 million shares outstanding. Assume each dollar raised increases company value by one dollar. How many new shares should it issue? What should be the target price?

$$NS = \frac{\$2M \times 1.2M}{\$10M}$$

$$= 0.24M \text{ shares}$$

$$\text{Target Price} = \frac{\$10M + \$2M}{1.2M + .24M}$$

$$= \$8.33 \text{ per share}$$

Equations (11.31) and (11.32) are controversial because there is no guarantee funds raised will be as productive as funds already invested in the company. The number of shares a company should issue and the Target Price per share is probably bracketed by the two versions of this equation.

Concentration Ratios

When an investment bank advises a client on a merger, it must take into account the regulatory environment. The Sherman Anti-Trust Act makes mergers in restraint of trade a felony. One indicator of whether a merger will restrain trade is how concentrated the industry is now, and how much more concentrated it will be after the merger.

Concentration ratios ask questions like (i) What percent of the total market will be captured by the top four companies? (ii) What percent of the market will be captured by the top eight companies? The market is defined as the total sales of a particular product or service.

Market size is a function of how the market is defined. DuPont was the subject of an anti-trust action for dominating the cellophane market. DuPont successfully argued the relevant market was for food-wraps which included cellophane (plastic wrap), wax paper, and butcher's paper *United States v. E. I Dupont* 351 US 377 (1956). DuPont had a tiny fraction of the market as they defined it. The Federal Trade Commission and the Justice Department decide whether mergers would tend to give the merged company monopoly power.

The formula for Concentration-4 and Concentration-8 is given in equations (11.33) and (11.34).

$$\text{Concentration-4} = \sum_{1}^{4} \text{Market}_i / \sum_{1}^{n} \text{Market}_i \qquad (11.33)$$

$$\text{Concentration-8} = \sum_{1}^{8} \text{Market}_i / \sum_{1}^{n} \text{Market}_i \qquad (11.34)$$

Where Concentration-4 is the share of the market captured by the top four companies and Concentration-8 is the share of the market captured by the top eight companies. The Greek symbol Σ means sum, or add up, all the items to the right of Σ beginning at the item number below Σ and ending with the item number above the Σ. So for Concentration-4 add up sales starting with the top selling company, number 1, and continue adding to the fourth largest company by sales. Summing from 1 to n means add up the sales of all the companies in the relevant market where n is the number of such companies.

Suppose the market were composed of companies with sales in millions of $50, $40, $30, $20, $15, $10, $8, $6, $4, $3, $3, $2, $2, $2.

$$\text{Concentration-4} = \frac{\$50 + \$40 + \$30 + \$20}{\$50 + \$40 + \$30 + \$20 + \$15 + \$10 + \$8 + \$6 + \$4 + \$3 + \$3 + \$2 + \$2 + \$2}$$

$$= \$140 / \$195$$

$$= 71.8\%$$

The Concentration ratio is always reported as a percent. With the top four companies garnering almost 72% of sales, mergers among the top four companies probably wouldn't be allowed, and mergers between any one of the top four and the next level companies would probably also be disallowed. However, mergers between companies with $15 million or less would probably be allowed.

Herfindahl Index

The Herfindahl Index is another means of measuring whether a merger is likely to give a company monopoly power. The Herfindahl Index is generated by (i) multiplying the market share of each company by 100, (ii) squaring the resulting number, and (iii) adding the squared numbers together. If the largest company had less than 1% of the market share, the process would result in squaring numbers less than 1, which tends to make them smaller. The resulting Herfindahl index would be very small. On the other hand, where there was a perfect monopoly, the monopoly company would have 100% of the market share, times 100 and then squaring the result would give a Herfindahl Index of 10,000. Generally, if a merger would generate a Herfindahl Index greater than about 1,800 or would increase the index by more than 400, it will receive increased scrutiny from regulators.

The formula for the Herfindahl Index is given as equation (11.35).

$$\text{Herfindahl Index} = \sum_{1}^{n} (M_i \times 100)^2 \tag{11.35}$$

Where Mi is the percentage of market captured by company i, and n is the number of companies in the industry.

Suppose the market were composed of companies whose sales in millions were $50, $40, $30, $20, $15, $10, $8, $6, $4, $3, $3, $2, $2, $2. Their respective share of the total market would be 25.6%, 20.5%, 15.4%, 10.3%, 7.7%, 5.1%, 4.1%, 3.1%, 2.1%, 1.5%, 1.5%, 1.03% 1.03% and 1.03%. Multiplying each by 100 and squaring them gives

$$= 655.4 + 420.8 + 236.7 + 105.2 + 59.3 + 26.3 + 16.8$$
$$+ 9.6 + 4.2 + 2.4 + 2.4 + 1.1 + 1.1 + 1.1$$

$$= 1,542.4$$

This would not be considered a highly concentrated industry. However, if the second and third companies merged, the merged company would have $70 million in combined sales and about 35.9% of the total market. The post merger Herfandahl Index would be

$$= 1,288.8 + 655.4 + 105.2 + 59.3 + 26.3 + 16.8$$
$$+ 9.6 + 4.2 + 2.4 + 2.4 + 1.1. + 1.1 + 1.1$$

$$= 2,173.7$$

The merger of the second and third largest companies in this industry would probably bring increased scrutiny under the over 1,800 rule and under the increase of 400 rule. The Federal Trade Commission and the Justice Department both have the statutory authority to prevent such a merger.

Recapitalization

Capitalization refers to how assets are financed. The only two options for financing assets are debt and equity. One of the things investment banks do to improve shareholder value is to examine whether a company has an appropriate level of debt. If a company has excess debt, interest related to that debt is a drag on company performance and increases the risk of failure during periodic economic downturns.

On the other hand, some companies have below average debt and above average cash flow. This creates an opportunity to return equity to shareholders and replace equity capital with debt.

Suppose a company has a Debt Service Coverage Ratio of 5 when the industry average Debt Service Coverage Ratio is 3. How much more principal and interest could a company service without falling below the industry average? Debt Service Coverage Ratio is given by equation (11.36). Let Interest Expense, Loan Principal, Operating Lease Payments, Capital Lease Payments and Sinking Fund Payments be replaced by Current Debt Service, substitute Target Debt Service Coverage for Debt Service coverage, and add a new variable in the denominator called New Debt Service to get equation (11.37). Equation (11.37) can be rewritten as equation (11.38).

$$\text{Debt Service Coverage} = \frac{\text{EBIT}}{\substack{\text{Interest Expense} + \text{Loan Principal} \\ + \text{Operating Lease Payments} + \text{Capital Lease Payments} \\ + \text{Sinking Fund Payments}}} \quad (11.36)$$

$$\substack{\text{Target Debt} \\ \text{Service Coverage}} = \frac{\text{EBIT}}{\text{Current Debt Service} + \text{New Debt Service}} \quad (11.37)$$

$$\text{New Debt Service} = \frac{\text{EBIT}}{\text{Target Debt Service Coverage}} - \text{Current Debt Service} \quad (11.38)$$

Suppose a company has an EBIT of $1,000, Current Debt Service of $200 and a Target Debt Service of 3. How much New Debt Service can it carry? Applying equation (11.38),

$$= \frac{\$1,000}{3} - \$200$$

$$= \$333.3 - \$200$$

$$= \$133.3$$

Translating New Debt Service into debt, which translates dollar for dollar into the amount of equity shareholders can pay out to themselves is tricky. It depends on the cost of debt to this particular company and whether the debt is going to be relatively short term, for example a three year bank loan or longer term, for example corporate bonds which are repaid over a period of ten, twenty or even thirty years.

Suppose the equity withdraw is financed with a ten year, 12% term loan. Payments will be made monthly which means the period interest rate k, will be 1% (12% per year /12 payments per year) and n is the number of payments (12 payments per year x 10 years). Twelve monthly payments must equal the annual increase in debt service of $133.3. That means that each monthly payment must equal $11.1 ($133.3 / 12 payments per year). Equation (11.39) provides the present value of all the new debt service payments, where PVIFA is the Present Value Interest Factor for an Annuity. See Appendices for PFIFA Tables.

$$\begin{aligned} PV &= \text{Payment} \times \text{PVIFA(k, n)} \quad (11.39) \\ &= \$11.1 \times \text{PVIFA(1\%, 120)} \\ &= \$11.1 \times 69.7005 \\ &= \$773.7 \end{aligned}$$

Based on this example, shareholders should be able to withdraw about $773.7 of equity from the company and replace it with debt without materially increasing the company's risk. A prudent investment banker would construct proforma financial statements replacing equity with debt and determine whether (i) the company's debt equity ratio was still within acceptable levels and (ii) the impact of the additional debt on the company's borrowing capacity.

Conclusion

Investment banks provide a number of services including mergers and acquisitions, valuations, underwriting IPOs and advice on maximizing shareholder value. There are a number of ways to value a company including market cap, book value, EBITDA multiplier method, Sales multiplier method, Net Income multiplier, discounted cash flow, Value per Customer and others. Publicly traded companies have registered their shares with the SEC, and such shares can be sold to anyone. Privately held companies have not registered their shares and therefore such shares cannot be resold. Inability to resell shares makes investments in private companies illiquid (hard to convert to cash). As a consequence, privately held companies usually sell at a discount of 25% to 30% to similar publicly traded companies.

Investment bankers help companies go public and suggest the price at which shares should be sold. Companies should independently estimate the price of new share issues.

Mergers and acquisitions are controlled by the federal government. When a merger threatens to significantly increase a company's monopoly power, the Federal Trade Commission or Justice Department can prohibit the merger. The government uses Concentration ratios and the Herfindahl Index to determine whether mergers are likely to give a firm monopoly power.

Investment banks also advise on maximizing shareholder wealth. One strategy for maximizing shareholder wealth is to recapitalize companies that have a higher than normal Debt Service Coverage Ratio and cash flow.

CHAPTER 12

Key Performance Indicators

Introduction

Key Performance Indicators (KPIs) generally have three characteristics (i) they may include non-financial data, (ii) they are aligned with someone's personal responsibility and (iii) they contribute to some financial goal. Key Performance Indicators quantify progress toward larger corporate goals. For example, if the managers of Wal-Mart stores were told the company's goal was to grow sales by $4 billion, what would they do? What would they be responsible for? How would they, as individuals, be measured and rewarded?

On the other hand, if the goal were to grow same store sales by 6%, that is something each one of them can be held accountable for. This goal can be broken down into sub-goals, for example, increase store traffic (the number of people visiting the store) and conversions (the number of visitors who purchase something). So, three of a store manager's KPIs would be (i) increase year over year sales, (ii) increase traffic, and (iii) increase conversions.

With quantitative data in hand, stores can be compared to each other and to historical performance. Underperforming stores can be targeted for training, change of management or even closure and high performing stores can be studied to find tools and techniques that can be used in other stores.

Many key performance indicators are unique to particular industries. The KPIs discussed in this chapter are illustrative, but not exhaustive. Trade journals are an invaluable source of KPIs for a particular industry. Many journals are sponsored by trade associations. The *Encyclopedia of Associations*, available in most libraries, lists trade journals.

There is an unfortunate tendency in many companies to keep KPI information secret. A better approach is to make everyone's performance available to everyone else so they can see where they are. No one wants to be the last one around the track or even in the last half of the pack, so making performance measures widely available can stimulate performance.[1]

The balance of the chapter provides examples of key performance indicators used by various industries. It is meant to stimulate thinking about what can be measured and the objectives of such measures. Often a KPI from one industry is useful in another.

Aerospace, Defense and Government Contracts

Backlog to Sales

In aerospace and defense there is a long lead time between winning a contract and being able to book a sale. So it is important to know what is in the pipeline. Backlog, that is signed contracts for work is one measure of what is in the pipeline. Backlog can be measured in dollars of sales or estimated months of production.

Facility Cost per Square Foot

Many government contracts are based on cost plus fixed fee. To properly bill the government costs must be well known. Costs of facilities are generally allocated to contracts based on the square feet of space used so it is important to know the cost per square foot. Facility costs include physical plant, maintenance, utilities, insurance, property taxes, janitorial and security costs.

Airlines

Load Factor

Load factor is the percentage of seats occupied when a plane takes off. An airline's inventory is the seats it has on planes. Once a plane leaves the ground, empty seats become spoiled inventory.

Cost per Passenger Mile

Moving people efficiently is a key performance goal for airlines and one measure of that efficiency is cost per passenger mile.

---

1 *Stewart, Thomas A., and Louise O'Brien. 2005. "Execution Without Excuses," Harvard Business Review. March. pp.102-111,105.*

On Time Arrivals

On time arrivals is the number of flights that arrive within ten minutes of scheduled arrival time divided by total flights. On Time Arrivals helps drive customer satisfaction and greater ticket sales.

Turnaround Time

Turnaround time is the time it takes to refuel, clean up and prepare a plane to fly again. The shorter the turnaround time, the more time a plane can be in the air generating revenue.

Auto Manufacturing

Hours per Vehicle Assembly

The number of hours needed to produce a vehicle including assembly, stamping and power train manufacture is an important measure of efficiency. This information is routinely compiled and published in the Harbour Report by Oliver Wyman.

Contribution per Vehicle

Contribution per Vehicle is the amount that each vehicle contributes to covering fixed costs such as plant, equipment, and administrative expenses. Company contribution is the weighted average of the Contribution per Vehicle, so increasing the contribution of each vehicle and producing more high contribution vehicles (assuming they can be sold) increases a company's overall contribution.

Percentage of vehicles that pass final inspection

This is a simple unit percentage. Increasing this to nearly 100% is important because pulling a failed auto off the assembly line for rework is very expensive.

Warranty Claims

Warranty claims in the first 90 days and warranty claims over the life of a vehicle's warranty are both KPIs that directly affect consumer loyalty, future sales and the cost of warranty claims and repairs.

Auto Dealers

Days of inventory

A key performance indicator for dealerships is the number of days of unsold inventory they have. This measure informs pricing policy, new orders from manufacturers and the mix of autos ordered.

Dealers Needed to Make 1% of Sales

This is an important means of evaluating a dealer network. If there are too many small dealers, they will not be able to keep up with technological advances in auto repair; competition among dealers selling the same product will prevent them from maximizing price which limits the amount manufacturers can charge dealers; and small dealers might not have enough critical mass to break even which places additional credit and collection burdens on manufacturers.

Banks

Banks make ratios out of everything. It is beyond the scope of this book to discuss them all. Ratios and data for banks are available at the website www2.fdic.gov/ubpr/UbprReport/SearchEngine/Default.asp. A few ratios peculiar to banks are discussed below.[2]

Rate Paid on Funds

Rate Paid on Funds is Total Interest Expense divided by Total Earning Assets. It is a measure of the cost of funds. If this gets too high it can signal trouble. However, a bank with a lower than average Rate Paid on Funds may return above average performance.

Net Interest Margin (NIM)

Net Interest Margin is the average rate of interest produced by Earning Assets less the Rate Paid on Funds.

Delinquency Rate

If principal and interest on a loan are not paid when due, the loan is said to be delinquent. Lateness of one or two days may not signal that a loan is headed for default, but substantial lateness does. Delinquency rate is the number of loans for which principal and interest is overdue by more than 30 days divided by the total number of loans.

---

2 __. 2009. "US Business Reporter, Understanding Bank Ratios," Jan. 15. www.activemedia-guide.com/busedu_banking.htm.

Reserve as a Percentage of Loans

Reserve as a Percentage of Loans is the Total Reserves in dollars divided by the Total Loans in dollars. Reserves represent outstanding loans a bank suspects it cannot collect. Reserves are similar to an Allowance for Doubtful Accounts for a non-bank company.

Charge-offs as a Percentage of Loans

Charge-offs are loans that a bank is certain it cannot collect and which it removes from both its loans and reserves. Charge-offs as a Percentage of Loans is computed by dividing the amount of loans charged off by the total value of the loan portfolio. As it increases, Reserves should increase. Increasing reserves decreases net income.

Long Term Debt to Total Liabilities and Equity

The ratio Long Term Debt to Total Liabilities and Equity could be rewritten as is Long Term Debt to Assets since Assets are equal to Liabilities plus Equity. Long term debt is debt maturing more than a year after the statement date. Banks borrow money from each other all the time. However, as this ratio rises, it will be more and more difficult for a bank to borrow funds from other banks.

Loans to Assets

Loans to Assets is Total Loans divided by Total Assets. Loans generate interest income where as assets like buildings, furniture and fixtures do not generate income.

Loans to Deposits

Loans to Deposits is Total Loans divided by Deposits. This ratio should be high as possible, but a certain amount of each deposit must be held as a reserve. On the other hand, loans can be funded by equity so the Loans to Deposits ratio could be greater than 100%.

Equity to Assets

Equity to Assets is Shareholder Equity divided by Average Total Assets. Shareholder equity provides a cushion for those lending to banks in the sense that losses will be charged against equity first, and only then will losses impair the value of loans to banks.

Non-Current Loan Ratio

The non-current loan ratio is the value of loans not timely paying principal and interest divided by total loans.

Colleges – *See Universities*

Construction

Construction has many measures some of which duplicate those of manufacturing or other fields. Some that are unique to construction are included below.[3]

Labor Productivity

Labor Productivity can be expressed as the ratio of the estimated labor used on a job divided by the actual labor used. A higher productivity ratio is better than a lower ratio. If a job uses less labor than estimated the ratio will be over 1.0. If more labor is used than estimated the ratio will be less than 1.0 meaning labor was less productive than anticipated.

Scheduling Variance

Scheduling Variance is the difference between the estimated date of completion and the actual date of completion. Minimizing scheduling variance is important in keeping clients satisfied and in scheduling deployment of equipment, materials and labor.

Unapproved Order Changes

Unapproved order changes can arise because clients change their specifications or construction personnel adapt to unanticipated changes in conditions or resources. An unapproved order usually implies the customer has not agreed to pay any increased cost. Minimizing unrecoverable cost is a key to construction profitability.

Customer Satisfaction Scorecard

Customer satisfaction is the key to getting paid, getting more work from the customer, as well as referrals and word of mouth advertising. Many factors contribute to customer satisfaction; the specific factors surveyed will depend on the type of construction involved. Homeowners might value courteous workers who clean up the worksite when the job is done. Commercial customers might value debris removal and re-grading the

3   Scott, Robert W. 2008. "Putting Data to Work," Accounting Technology. June. pp.36-37.

ground around the construction site. Every customer values jobs that are completed on time and on budget.

Bid Win Ratio

Construction companies usually have to bid to for large commercial and government contracts. The number of times they win a bid divided by the number of bids submitted is the Bid Win Ratio. A very high ratio may mean a company is under pricing contracts. A very low ratio may mean it is overpricing contracts.

Hotels

Hotels have their own key performance indicators, some of which are discussed below.[4]

Occupancy Rate

Occupancy Rate is Rooms Sold divided by Total Rooms Available.

Average Daily Rate

Average Daily Rate is the Dollar Value of Sales divided by Number of Rooms Sold. Rooms do not always rent for a standard rate. When demand is high the standard rate is charged. When occupancy is low, hotels charge less than the standard rate to fill rooms. Discounts are also given to members of groups.

Revenue per Available Rooms

Revenue per Available Rooms is the Dollar Value of Sales divided by the Total Number of Rooms Available. Some argue this is a more accurate view of profitability than Average Daily Rate.

Yield Ratio

Yield Management is the trade-off between setting a low price and getting high occupancy or holding out for the standard rate and accepting a lower occupancy rate. The Yield Ratio is Sales divided by Total Theoretical Sales if all rooms were sold at the standard rate.

---

4   Patterson, Richard F. 2008. "Yield Management and Performance Ratios." March 30. www.wku.edu/~rich. patterson/CFS-171/171ntc10.htm

Insurance

Renewal Rate

The renewal rate is the percentage of policies that renew every year. If the renewal rate exceeds some threshold, say 85%, that is a signal that there may be an opportunity to raise price. If the renewal rate slips below some threshold, say 60%, that might be a signal that policies are overpriced.

Claims Ratio

Claims ratio is the ratio of the dollar value of claims to written premiums for a particular line of business. The claims ratio includes both actual claim payments and anticipated claims that will eventually filed for the year based on historical statistics. For example, an accident may occur December 26th, but may not be reported until January 2nd of the following year. Anticipated claims are called Incurred But Not Reported (IBNR). The claims ratio includes the cost of litigation designed to avoid paying a claim. A high claims ratio may mean a company is insuring too many risky clients or that premiums are not high enough for the risk involved.

Expense Ratio

The expense ratio is all the expenses involved in servicing a line of insurance divided by policy premiums. Expenses include the cost of underwriting a policy (calculating risk and determining the premium to charge), issuing the policy and collecting premiums.

Combined Ratio

The combined ratio is the Claims Ratio plus the Expense Ratio for a particular line of business. If it is consistently higher than 100%, that may signal that a particular line of business, state or industry is unprofitable.

Internet

Page Views

Page Views is the number of times someone navigates to a particular web page. Arguably if a webpage attracts a large number of visitors it becomes a valuable property. Counters can be built into web pages to count visitors.

Dwell Time

Dwell Time is the number of seconds a visitor spends on a particular web page, or web site. Arguably the more interesting the content, the longer someone will spend on a page. Dwell time increases a page's value as a billboard.

Click Through

Those advertising on a company's webpage often have a webpage of their own they want potential customers to navigate to. By counting the number times a user viewing a page clicks through to the advertiser's page the customer can get a measure of whether it is worthwhile to advertise on the original page.

Purchases

Ultimately, a webpage's real value measure is how much is purchased as the result of the initial navigation to that webpage. A company that can capture Page Views, Dwell Time, Click Throughs, and Purchases can tell his or her advertisers how efficient its advertising dollars will be.

Magazines

Cancellation Rate

The cancellation rate is the percentage of total subscriptions canceling in one year. It is total cancellations divided by total circulation. A cancellation rate higher than industry norms may mean the magazine has lost appeal to its target audience and needs to be refocused. If the cancellation rate is consistently higher than the rate new subscribers are added, circulation will decline and with it advertising revenue.

Manufacturing

Repeat Sales

Repeat sales is the key to building any business. If a customer buys once and never buys again that means a company must find new customers all the time. Some experts believe it costs five times as much to find and sell to a new customer as it does to sell to an existing customer. The measure of repeat sales will differ for every industry and type of good. Repeat sales can be measured as the percentage of sales from existing customers.

Customer Life

Customer Life is the average time between gaining and losing a customer. Everything has a life cycle including customers. At some point customers will become bored with a company's products or a competitor will offer something new. One measure of how a company is doing is to measure the amount of time between winning a customer and losing a customer. If a customer's pattern is to purchase goods monthly, and then it doesn't purchase for three months, that customer has been lost. The customer is at the end of its life. It must be re-won, or another customer must be won to take its place. Short customer life indicates a company is not providing good customer satisfaction.

Lead Generation

Companies like Dell tract lead generation.[5] Each company must define what they consider a lead. For example, in industrial sales a lead may be identification of a new customer and the relevant customer contact. In other companies, to qualify as a lead, the customer might have to do something like schedule a meeting with the potential customer's purchasing manager.

New Products

Some companies bring a target number of new products to market each year. Other companies measure sales from new products and set targets of generating 10% to 20% of sales from new products each year.

Operating Expenses to Gross Margin

Hewlett Packard tracks operating expenses as a percent of gross margin.[6] This helps assure that overhead is strictly controlled.

Warranty Claims

Most goods are sold with warranties. A key performance indicator for any manufacturer is the total number of warranty claims. This might be measured in claims per hundred thousand units.

---

5 Stewart, Thomas A., and Louise O'Brien. 2005. "Execution Without Excuses," Harvard Business Review. March. pp.102-111,107.
6 Kaihla, Paul and Patrick Baltatzis, Harris Collingwood, Michael Copeland, Bridget Finn, Susanna Hamner, David Jacobson, Jeff Nachtigal, Erick Schonfeld, Paul Sloan, Owen Thomas. 2006. "Best Kept Secrets of the World's Best Companies," Business 2.0. Apr. Vol.7 Iss.3 pp82-96.

On the Job Injuries

Many manufacturing companies post the number of days of operations without an injury that causes lost work. This measure helps make employees aware of safety. Increased safety reduces Workers Compensation claims.

Refineries

Yield

Yield is the number of gallons of a product a refinery can get from a barrel of crude oil. The products with the highest value usually have the most closely watched yield. For example, a refinery could monitor the yield of diesel fuel, the yield of gasoline, and other products. Yield is also applied to semi-conductor manufacturing for example in the yield of perfectly working chips that can be produced from a wafer of silicon. Other industries use the concept of yield as well.

Days in Inventory

An important indicator of whether gasoline prices are likely to rise or fall is the number of days supply in inventory. It is the total inventory divided by the daily usage.

Retail

Retail key performance indicators (KPIs) are designed to break sales and profit improvement targets into manageable goals.

Same Store Sales

Same Store Sales is the change in sales from year to year divided by the prior year's sales. Stores that chronically under perform may be targeted for rehabilitation, change of management or closure.

Daily Sales

This is the sales on every day of the year. To make this report meaningful, the prior year's sales for the same day should be presented in a side by side comparison. The same-day-prior year should be adjusted so that Monday's compare with Monday's and Saturday's with Saturdays.

Some companies track sales hourly. Dell monitors order activity in real time and if fewer than expected orders come in by 10:00 AM, they run a special on their website by 10:15 AM.[7]

---

7   Stewart, Thomas A., and Louise O'Brien. 2005. "Execution Without Excuses," Harvard Business Review.

Traffic

This is the number of visitors to the store whether or not they purchase anything. Traffic can be counted with an electric eye if a store separates entering and leaving traffic. The more visitors, the greater the possibility of sales. Traffic should be reported daily with the same-day-prior year traffic reported for comparative purposes.

Conversion Rate

This is the percentage of visitors who purchase something. The conversion rate can be estimated by dividing the number of purchases captured from cash registers by the traffic count. Conversion can be improved by having the goods or services a customer wants in stock and placed where they are easy to find. Conversion should be tracked weekly or monthly. Annual tracking is too coarse a measure to be useful.

Fill Rate

Fill rate is the percentage of time a vendor has a desired item in stock.[8] Fill rate places an upper limit on conversions. Some estimate that 15% to 25% of retail sales are lost because customers cannot find the item they are looking for or it is out of stock.

Average Purchase

The Average Purchase is sales dollars divided by the number of sales. Increasing the average purchase by even a small amount can significantly increase total sales. One approach is to place impulse items and sale items near cash registers.

Average Gross Margin per Sale

Some retail items have a high gross margin; some have a very slim gross margin. The more high margin products a store sells the more profitable it will be. Unless Gross Margin per sale is measured and reported as a key performance indicator managers will not focus on this element of profit. Most retail sales are scanned. This enables retailers to look up both the sales price and the cost of the good being sold which can be used to compute Gross Margin per Sale.

Sales per Square Foot

Real estate is expensive so it is important to know whether space is being efficiently used. Sales per square foot is one measure of space utilization efficiency. While the

---

March. pp.102-111,105.
8   Harvard Business School (HBS) Case Matching Dell 9-799-158 p.10

number of square feet in a facility changes only rarely, sales change all the time so this measure should probably be computed and reported weekly or monthly.

Sales per Dollar of Rent

Sales per dollar of rent is designed to help a company understand whether there is a payoff in placing stores in expensive malls or shopping pavilions as opposed to stand alone stores or strip malls, in low income towns versus high income towns and so forth. Since store placement decisions are only made or revised over long time frames, a monthly or quarterly report of Sales per Dollar of Rent is probably sufficient.

Store Asset Turnover

Store asset turnover is similar to company level asset turnover. It is sales divided by the assets needed to run a store. Store assets include leasehold improvements, furniture, fixtures, equipment and inventory. Corporate probably decides on a store's leasehold improvements, furniture, fixtures and equipment which places these items beyond the control of a store manager. But inventory and sales are variables each store manager can control. Selecting better, more salable inventory goes a long way toward optimizing Store Asset Turnover.

Annual or even quarterly reports are not useful for execution management because they are not timely. Even monthly reports have limited value. Many successful companies like Dow Chemical and Boeing measure performance on a weekly basis which forces everyone to "live the details of execution."[9]

Sales & Marketing

Advertising Effectiveness

It has been said that half of all advertising is wasted; the problem is knowing which half. Advertising effectiveness is a key performance indicator that can help determine which half is wasted. All advertising should be done with some specific measure of effectiveness in mind. The simplest example is to advertise a product with a coupon in the advertisement. The number of coupons redeemed will provide a direct measure of the effectiveness of the advertisement.

CPK

Calls per thousand of media expenditures (CPK) is a specific measure of advertising effectiveness where television advertisements are linked to call center phone numbers.

---

9 Mankins, Michael C. and Richard Steele. 2005. "Turning Great Strategy into Great Performance," Harvard Business Review. Jul.-Aug. pp.65-72,72.

Some advertising agencies claim they can drive a certain number of CPKs with their ads.[10]

Complaints

Complaint tracking is a key performance indicator for management because it can be used to spot trends in quality, service or even to identify individuals with poor training and attitude. Complaints should be scaled by some easy to understand denominator such as complaints per week, complaints per month, complaints per thousand customers, or complaints per thousand customers per week. Complaints should also capture the individual, product, service, cost or delay that is being complained of.

Acquisition Cost

Acquisition cost is the cost to acquire a new customer. It is total selling and marketing expenses divided by the number of new customers.

Telecommunications

Number of Subscribers

The number of subscribers is an important key performance indicator because the growth or decline in this measure can presage a company's future performance.

Revenue per Subscriber

Revenue per subscriber is an important measure because multiplied by the number of subscribers it becomes total revenue. Optimizing both the number of subscribers and the revenue per subscriber is important in optimizing revenue. Revenue per subscriber is also a factor in valuing a telecommunications company.

Market Value per Customer

One of the factors discussed in valuing a company is the Market Value per Customer. When Adelphia Communications was in bankruptcy its expected price was about $17 billion which would put a value of $3,200 on each customer. By contrast Comcast, the nation's largest cable company had a value per customer of $2,900. There was speculation that Comcast wouldn't offer $3,200 per customer, but would consider $3,000 per customer giving Adelphia a value of about $15.9 billion.[11]

---

10 Joel. 2008 "Managing by Metrics," KPI Direct Blog. May 27th. www.kpidirect.com/blog
11 Philadelphia Inquirer, Friday September 25, 2004, p.C6.

Investment per subscriber

One of the things that T. Rowe Price evaluates cable companies on is their investment per subscriber.[12] There are at least three ways to evaluate investment per subscriber (i) assets divided by the number of subscribers, (ii) plant, property and equipment divided by the number of subscribers and (iii) equity per subscriber.

Churn Rate

The Churn Rate is the percentage of subscribers who un-subscribe during a given period of time. Churn rate can be quoted per month, quarter or year. A high churn rate may mean the service is not competitive with other services in terms of price, quality or features.

Trucking

Profit per load

One mid-west trucking company executive scrutinizes the profit on each load hauled including things like distance, route, load factor, etc. His company has three times the industry average profit margin.

Universities

Student Faculty Ratio

The Student Faculty Ratio is the number of students divided by the number of faculty. It is one measure of how much personal attention each student might receive. This ratio can be deceptive because at many well know universities, there are research only faculty that do not teach and at some large universities faculty are only required to teach one or two courses per semester. The balance of the courses are taught by graduate students or adjunct (part time) faculty.

Admit Rate

The Admit Rate is the ratio of students admitted to the number of students who apply to the school. It is a measure of exclusivity.

Admit Coming Ratio

The Admit Coming ratio is the number of students who register divided by the number who were admitted. Most students apply to several colleges and then select among those which admit them.

12 Diya Gullapalli. "Sluething Boosts Fund's Retruns," Wall Street Journal. Aug. 5, 2005 p.C1.

Coming Attend Ratio

Not every student who registers for college actually attends. The Coming Attend ratio is the ratio of those who attend on the first day divided by those who register.

First Day Attend to Complete Ratio

The First Day Attend to Complete Ratio is the ratio of those who complete their freshman courses to those who come on the first day of class. Many students go to college to please family and friends, but quickly realize they don't have the discipline or drive to complete the coursework.

Graduation Rate

Graduation rate is the ratio of those who start college to those who graduate. This ratio is difficult to compute because many students transfer among colleges and not all students graduate in four years. The graduation rate is usually calculated as the percentage of entering freshmen who graduate within five years.

Utilities

Reliability

A key factor in a successful utility is the percentage of time it can fully service its customers. For an electric utility, Reliability is the amount of time electricity is actually available divided by the amount of time it is theoretically available. Suppose the electric is out for three days due to a hurricane. The total time electric should be available 8,760 hours per year (24 hours/day x 365 days). It was unavailable for 72 hours (3 days x 24 hours/day). Reliability is 99.12% ((8,760 – 72) / 8,760).

Capital per Customer

Capital per Customer is a measure of the assets needed to service each customer. Increasing the Capital per Customer faster than net income will drive Return on Assets and Return on Equity down. Capital per Customer is also important when evaluating the purchase of another utility or selling part of a utility's grid.

Capital per Unit of Production

Capital per Unit of Production is a measure of the efficiency of management in producing each unit of a utility's service. Units of service could be megawatts, thousands of cubic feet of natural gas, or the number of phone, cable or fiber optic lines.

Conclusion

Key Performance Indicators (KPIs) are industry specific measures used to set goals, control operations and measure results. KPI's may include financial as well as non-financial data. They are used to deconstruct large goals into smaller, more manageable goals. One characteristic of KPI's is that they can be used to hold employees accountable for specific aspects of a company's performance.

While many key performance indicators are industry specific, examining performance indicators in one industry might generate ideas for new performance indicators in other industries.

Appendixes

Appendix A: FVIF

Appendix B: PVIF

Appendix C: FVIFA

Appendix D: PVIFA

Appendix A: FVIF - Period Interest Rates

n	0.3333%	0.4167%	0.50%	0.75%	1.00%	1.25%	1.50%	2.00%	3.00%	4.00%	5.00%
1	1.0033333	1.004166667	1.005	1.0075	1.01	1.0125	1.015	1.02	1.03	1.04	1.05
2	1.006677711	1.008350695	1.010025	1.01505625	1.0201	1.02515625	1.030225	1.0404	1.0609	1.0816	1.1025
3	1.01003327	1.012552156	1.015075125	1.022669172	1.030301	1.037970703	1.045678375	1.061208	1.092727	1.124864	1.157625
4	1.013400014	1.016771123	1.020150501	1.030339191	1.04060401	1.050945337	1.061363551	1.08243216	1.12550881	1.16985856	1.21550625
5	1.01677798	1.02100767	1.025251253	1.038606735	1.05101005	1.064082154	1.077284004	1.104080803	1.159274074	1.216652902	1.276281563
6	1.020167206	1.025261868	1.030377509	1.045852235	1.061520151	1.077383181	1.093443264	1.126162419	1.194052297	1.265319018	1.340095641
7	1.023567729	1.029533793	1.035529397	1.053696127	1.072135352	1.09085047	1.109844913	1.148685668	1.229873865	1.315931779	1.407100423
8	1.026979588	1.033823517	1.040707044	1.061598848	1.082856706	1.104486101	1.126492587	1.171659381	1.266770081	1.36856905	1.477455444
9	1.030402819	1.038131115	1.045910579	1.069560839	1.093685273	1.118292177	1.143389975	1.195092569	1.304773184	1.423311812	1.551328216
10	1.03383746	1.042456661	1.051140132	1.077582545	1.104622125	1.13227083	1.160540825	1.21899442	1.343916379	1.480244285	1.628894627
11	1.037283551	1.046800231	1.056395833	1.085664415	1.115668347	1.146424215	1.177948937	1.243374308	1.384233871	1.539454056	1.710339358
12	1.040741128	1.051161898	1.061677812	1.093806898	1.12682503	1.160754518	1.195618171	1.268241795	1.425760887	1.601032219	1.795856326
13	1.04421023	1.05554174	1.066986201	1.102010449	1.13809328	1.175263949	1.213552444	1.29360663	1.468533713	1.665073507	1.885649142
14	1.047690896	1.05993983	1.072321132	1.110275528	1.149474213	1.189954749	1.231755731	1.319478763	1.512589725	1.731676448	1.979931599
15	1.051183164	1.064356246	1.077682738	1.118602594	1.160968955	1.204829183	1.250232067	1.345868338	1.557967417	1.800943506	2.078928179
16	1.054687073	1.068791064	1.083071151	1.126992114	1.172578645	1.219889548	1.268985548	1.372785705	1.604706439	1.872981246	2.182874588
18	1.061729969	1.077716212	1.09392894	1.143960389	1.196147476	1.250577394	1.307340636	1.428246248	1.702433061	2.025816515	2.406619234
20	1.068819894	1.08671589	1.104895577	1.161184142	1.22019004	1.282037232	1.346855007	1.485947396	1.806111235	2.191123143	2.653297705
24	1.083142096	1.104941336	1.127159776	1.196413529	1.269734649	1.34735105	1.429502812	1.608437249	2.032794106	2.563304165	3.225099944
28	1.097656214	1.123472444	1.14987261	1.232711748	1.321290967	1.415992304	1.51722218	1.741024206	2.287927676	2.998703319	3.920129138
30	1.104986045	1.132854219	1.161400083	1.251271764	1.347848915	1.45161336	1.56308022	1.811361584	2.427262471	3.24339751	4.321942375
32	1.112364823	1.142314338	1.173043119	1.270111224	1.374940679	1.488130509	1.61032432	1.884540592	2.575082756	3.508058747	4.764941469
36	1.127270526	1.161472233	1.196680525	1.308645371	1.430768784	1.563943819	1.709139538	2.039887344	2.898278328	4.103932554	5.791816136
40	1.142375967	1.180951427	1.220794236	1.348348612	1.488863734	1.643619463	1.814018409	2.208039664	3.262037792	4.801020628	7.039988712
48	1.173196799	1.220895357	1.270489161	1.431405333	1.612226078	1.815354853	2.043478289	2.587070385	4.132251879	6.570528242	10.40126965
50	1.181031068	1.231090681	1.283225815	1.45295693	1.644631822	1.861022374	2.105242421	2.691588029	4.383906019	7.106683346	11.46739979
60	1.22099416	1.283358681	1.348850153	1.565681027	1.816696699	2.107181347	2.443219776	3.281030788	5.891603104	10.51962741	18.67918589
72	1.270730839	1.349017747	1.432044278	1.712552707	2.047099312	2.445920268	2.921157961	4.161140375	8.400017267	16.84226241	33.54513415
84	1.322510173	1.418036056	1.520369636	1.873201963	2.306722744	2.839113001	3.49258954	5.277332137	11.97641607	26.96500475	60.24224138
96	1.376390729	1.490585473	1.614142708	2.048921228	2.599272926	3.295513243	4.175803519	6.69293318	17.07550559	43.17184138	108.1864103
108	1.43246644	1.566846655	1.713699499	2.241124172	2.928925793	3.825281884	4.992666568	8.488257586	24.345588	69.11950898	194.2872493
120	1.490826739	1.647009504	1.819396734	2.451357078	3.300386895	4.440213229	5.969322872	10.76516303	34.71098714	110.6625608	348.9119857
240	2.222564365	2.712640307	3.310204476	6.009151524	10.89255365	19.71549352	35.63281555	115.8887352	1204.852628	12246.20236	121739.5737
360	3.313458385	4.467744367	6.022575212	14.73057612	35.94964133	87.54099514	212.7037809	1247.561128	41821.62407	1355196.114	

6.00%	7.00%	8.00%	9.00%	10.00%	12.00%	15.00%	18.00%	20.00%	24.00%	30.00%
1.06	1.07	1.08	1.09	1.1	1.12	1.15	1.18	1.2	1.24	1.3
1.1236	1.1449	1.1664	1.1881	1.21	1.2544	1.3225	1.3924	1.44	1.5376	1.69
1.191016	1.225043	1.259712	1.295029	1.331	1.404928	1.520875	1.643032	1.728	1.906624	2.197
1.26247696	1.31079601	1.36048896	1.41158161	1.4641	1.57351936	1.74900625	1.93877776	2.0736	2.36421376	2.8561
1.338225578	1.402551731	1.469328077	1.538623955	1.61051	1.762341683	2.011357188	2.287757757	2.48832	2.931625062	3.71293
1.418519112	1.500730352	1.586874323	1.677100111	1.771561	1.973822685	2.313060766	2.699554153	2.985984	3.635215077	4.826809
1.503630259	1.605781476	1.713824269	1.828039121	1.9487171	2.210681407	2.66001988	3.185473901	3.5831808	4.507666696	6.2748517
1.593848075	1.71818618	1.85093021	1.992562642	2.14358881	2.475963176	3.059022863	3.758859203	4.29981696	5.589506703	8.15730721
1.689478959	1.838459212	1.999004627	2.171893279	2.357947691	2.773078757	3.517876292	4.435453859	5.159780352	6.930988312	10.60449937
1.790847697	1.967151357	2.158924997	2.367363675	2.59374246	3.105848208	4.045057736	5.233835554	6.191736422	8.594425506	13.78584918
1.898298558	2.104851952	2.331638997	2.580426405	2.853116706	3.478549993	4.652391396	6.175925953	7.430083707	10.65708763	17.92160394
2.012196472	2.252191589	2.518170117	2.812664782	3.138428377	3.895975993	5.350250105	7.287592625	8.916100448	13.21478866	23.29808512
2.13292826	2.409845	2.719623726	3.065804612	3.452271214	4.363493112	6.152787621	8.599359298	10.69932054	16.38633794	30.28751066
2.260903956	2.57853415	2.937193624	3.341727027	3.797498336	4.887112285	7.075705764	10.14724397	12.83918465	20.31905904	39.37376386
2.396558193	2.759031541	3.172169114	3.64248246	4.177248169	5.473565759	8.137061629	11.97374789	15.40702157	25.19563321	51.18589301
2.540351685	2.952163749	3.425942643	3.970305881	4.594972986	6.13039365	9.357620874	14.12902251	18.48842589	31.24258518	66.54166092
2.854339153	3.379932276	3.996019499	4.717120417	5.559917313	7.689965795	12.37545361	19.67325094	26.62333328	48.03859898	112.455407
3.207135472	3.869684462	4.660957144	5.604410768	6.727499949	9.646293093	16.36653739	27.3930346	38.33759992	73.86414979	190.0496377
4.048934641	5.072366953	6.341180737	7.911083175	9.849732676	15.17862893	28.62517619	53.10900627	79.4968472	174.6306393	542.8007704
5.111686697	6.648838364	8.627106386	11.16713952	14.42099361	23.88386649	50.06561207	102.9665602	164.8446624	412.8641603	1550.29328
5.743491173	7.612255043	10.06265689	13.26767847	17.44940227	29.95992212	66.21177196	143.3706384	237.3763138	634.8199329	2619.995644
6.453386682	8.715270798	11.737083	15.76332879	21.11377675	37.58172631	87.56506841	199.629277	341.8218919	976.0991289	4427.792638
8.147252	11.42394219	15.96817184	22.25122503	30.91268053	59.13557393	153.1518519	387.0368024	708.801875	2307.706992	12646.21855
10.28571794	14.97445784	21.7245215	31.40942005	45.25925557	93.05097044	267.8635462	750.3783448	1469.771568	5455.912624	36118.86481
16.39387173	25.72890651	40.21057314	62.585237	97.01723378	230.3907763	819.400712	2820.566547	6319.748715	30495.86018	294632.6763
18.42015427	29.45702506	46.90161251	74.35752008	117.3908529	289.0021898	1083.657442	3927.35686	9100.43815	46890.43461	497929.223
32.98769085	57.94642683	101.2570637	176.031292	304.4816395	897.5969335	4383.998746	20555.13997	56347.51435	402996.3473	6864377.173
66.37771515	130.5064551	254.9825118	495.1170154	955.5938177	3497.016104	23455.48975	149797.4864	502400.098	5325511.559	
133.5650042	293.9255405	642.0893416	1392.598192	2999.062754	13624.29079	125492.7365	1091663.057	4479449.739		
268.7590303	661.9766302	1616.890192	3916.91189	9412.343651	53079.90982	671417.5268	7955595.646			
540.7959725	1490.898199	4071.604565	11016.96013	29539.96641	206798.0543	3592251.693				
1088.187748	3357.788383	10252.99294	30987.01575	92709.06882	805680.255					
1184152.575										

165

Appendix B: PVIF - Period Interest Rates

n	0.3333%	0.4167%	0.50%	0.75%	1.00%	1.25%	1.50%	2.00%	3.00%	4.00%	5.00%
1	0.99667774	0.99585062	0.9950248	0.9925558	0.9900990	0.9876543	0.9852216	0.9803921	0.9708737	0.9615384	0.9523809
2	0.99336651	0.99171846	0.9900745	0.9851670	0.9802960	0.9754610	0.9706617	0.9611687	0.9425959	0.9245562	0.9070294
3	0.99006629	0.98760344	0.9851487	0.9778333	0.9705901	0.9634183	0.9563169	0.9423223	0.9151416	0.8889963	0.8638375
4	0.98677704	0.98350550	0.9802475	0.9705541	0.9609803	0.9515242	0.9421842	0.9238454	0.8884870	0.8548041	0.8227024
5	0.98349871	0.97942457	0.9753706	0.9633292	0.9514656	0.9397770	0.9282603	0.9057308	0.8626087	0.8219271	0.7835261
6	0.98023127	0.97536056	0.9705180	0.9561580	0.9420452	0.9281748	0.9145421	0.8879713	0.8374842	0.7903145	0.7462153
7	0.97697469	0.97131342	0.9656896	0.9490402	0.9327180	0.9167159	0.9010267	0.8705601	0.8130915	0.7599178	0.7106813
8	0.97372892	0.96728308	0.9608852	0.9419754	0.9234832	0.9053984	0.8877111	0.8534903	0.7894092	0.7306902	0.6768393
9	0.97049395	0.96326945	0.9561046	0.9349631	0.9143398	0.8942206	0.8745922	0.8367552	0.7664167	0.7025867	0.6446089
10	0.96726971	0.95927249	0.9513479	0.9280031	0.9052869	0.8831809	0.8616672	0.8203483	0.7440939	0.6755641	0.6139132
11	0.96405619	0.95529210	0.9466148	0.9210949	0.8963237	0.8722774	0.8489332	0.8042630	0.7224212	0.6495809	0.5846792
12	0.96085335	0.95132823	0.9419053	0.9142381	0.8874492	0.8615086	0.8363874	0.7884931	0.7013798	0.6245970	0.5568374
13	0.95766114	0.94738081	0.9372192	0.9074324	0.8786625	0.8508726	0.8240207	0.7730325	0.6809513	0.6005740	0.5303213
14	0.95447955	0.94344977	0.9325564	0.9006773	0.8699629	0.8403680	0.8118492	0.7578750	0.6611178	0.5774750	0.5050679
15	0.95130852	0.93953504	0.9279168	0.8939725	0.8613494	0.8299931	0.7998515	0.7430147	0.6418619	0.5552645	0.4810170
16	0.94814802	0.93563656	0.9233003	0.8873176	0.8528212	0.8197463	0.7880310	0.7284458	0.6231669	0.5339081	0.4581115
18	0.94185850	0.92788805	0.9141361	0.8741561	0.8360173	0.7996306	0.7649115	0.7001593	0.5873946	0.4936281	0.4155206
20	0.93561070	0.92020371	0.9050629	0.8611898	0.8195444	0.7800085	0.7424704	0.6729713	0.5536757	0.4563869	0.3768894
24	0.92323916	0.90502541	0.8871856	0.8358314	0.7875661	0.7421970	0.6995439	0.6217214	0.4919337	0.3901214	0.3100679
28	0.91103121	0.89009748	0.8696615	0.8112196	0.7568355	0.7062185	0.6590992	0.5743745	0.4370767	0.3334774	0.2550936
30	0.90498790	0.88272610	0.8610297	0.7991868	0.7419229	0.6888886	0.6397624	0.5520708	0.4119867	0.3083186	0.2313774
32	0.89898468	0.87541577	0.8524835	0.7873326	0.7273041	0.6719840	0.6209929	0.5306333	0.3883370	0.2850579	0.2098661
36	0.88709744	0.86097623	0.8356449	0.7641489	0.6989249	0.6394091	0.5850897	0.4902231	0.3450324	0.2436687	0.1726574
40	0.87536739	0.84677486	0.8191388	0.7416479	0.6716531	0.6084133	0.5512623	0.4528904	0.3065568	0.2082890	0.1420456
48	0.85237055	0.81907100	0.7870984	0.6986141	0.6202604	0.5508564	0.4893616	0.3865376	0.2419988	0.1521947	0.0961421
50	0.84671637	0.81228783	0.7792860	0.6882516	0.6080388	0.5373390	0.4750046	0.3715278	0.2281070	0.1407126	0.0872037
60	0.81900310	0.77920537	0.7413721	0.6386996	0.5504496	0.4745676	0.4092959	0.3047822	0.1697330	0.0950604	0.0535355
72	0.78694187	0.74128007	0.6983024	0.5839236	0.4884960	0.4088440	0.3423299	0.2403187	0.1190473	0.0593744	0.0298105
84	0.75613574	0.70520066	0.6577347	0.5338452	0.4335154	0.3522226	0.2863205	0.1894896	0.0834974	0.0370851	0.0165996
96	0.72653556	0.67087730	0.6195239	0.4880617	0.3847229	0.3034428	0.2394748	0.1494113	0.0585634	0.0231632	0.0092433
108	0.69809412	0.63822452	0.5835328	0.4462046	0.3414221	0.2614186	0.2002937	0.1178098	0.0410752	0.0144676	0.0051470
120	0.67076608	0.60716101	0.5496327	0.4079373	0.3029947	0.2252144	0.1675231	0.0928922	0.0288093	0.0090364	0.0028660
240	0.44992714	0.36864449	0.3020961	0.1664128	0.0918058	0.0507215	0.0280640	0.0086289	8.29977E-0		
360	0.30179586	0.22382656	0.1660419	0.0678860	0.0278166	0.0114232	0.0047013				

6.00%	7.00%	8.00%	9.00%	10.00%	12.00%	15.00%	18.00%	20.00%	24.00%	30.00%
0.9433962	0.9345794	0.9259259	0.9174311	0.9090909	0.8928571	0.8695652	0.8474576	0.83333333	0.8064516	0.7692307
0.8899964	0.8734387	0.8573388	0.8416799	0.8264462	0.7971938	0.7561436	0.7181844	0.69444444	0.6503642	0.5917159
0.8396192	0.8162978	0.7938322	0.7721834	0.7513148	0.7117802	0.6575162	0.6086308	0.57870370	0.5244872	0.4551661
0.7920936	0.7628952	0.7350298	0.7084252	0.6830134	0.6355180	0.5717532	0.5157888	0.48225308	0.4229735	0.3501277
0.7472581	0.7129861	0.6805831	0.6499313	0.6209213	0.5674268	0.4971767	0.4371092	0.40187757	0.3411077	0.2693290
0.7049605	0.6663422	0.6301696	0.5962673	0.5644739	0.5066311	0.4323275	0.3704315	0.33489797	0.2750868	0.2071762
0.6650571	0.6227497	0.5834903	0.5470342	0.5131581	0.4523492	0.3759370	0.3139250	0.27908164	0.2218442	0.1593663
0.6274123	0.5820091	0.5402688	0.5018662	0.4665073	0.4038832	0.3269017	0.2660381	0.23256803	0.1789066	0.1225894
0.5918984	0.5439337	0.5002489	0.4604277	0.4240976	0.3606100	0.2842624	0.2254560	0.19380669	0.1442795	0.0942995
0.5583947	0.5083492	0.4631934	0.4224108	0.3855432	0.3219732	0.2471847	0.1910644	0.16150558	0.1163544	0.0725381
0.5267875	0.4750927	0.4288828	0.3875328	0.3504938	0.2874761	0.2149432	0.1619190	0.13458798	0.0938342	0.0557985
0.4969693	0.4440119	0.3971137	0.3555347	0.3186308	0.2566750	0.1869071	0.1372195	0.11215665	0.0756727	0.0429219
0.4688390	0.4149644	0.3676979	0.3261786	0.2896643	0.2291741	0.1625279	0.1162877	0.09346387	0.0610264	0.0330169
0.4423009	0.3878172	0.3404610	0.2992464	0.2633312	0.2046198	0.1413286	0.0985489	0.07788656	0.0492148	0.0253976
0.4172650	0.3624460	0.3152417	0.2745380	0.2393920	0.1826962	0.1228944	0.0835160	0.06490547	0.0396894	0.0195366
0.3936462	0.3387345	0.2918904	0.2518697	0.2176291	0.1631216	0.1068647	0.0707763	0.05408789	0.0320075	0.0150281
0.3503437	0.2958639	0.2502490	0.2119937	0.1798587	0.1300395	0.0808051	0.0508304	0.03756103	0.0208165	0.0088924
0.3118047	0.2584190	0.2145482	0.1784308	0.1486436	0.1036667	0.0611002	0.0365056	0.02608405	0.0135383	0.0052617
0.2469785	0.1971466	0.1576993	0.1264049	0.1015255	0.0658821	0.0349342	0.0188291	0.01257911	0.0057263	0.0018422
0.1956301	0.1504022	0.1159137	0.0895484	0.0693433	0.0418692	0.0199737	0.0097118	0.00606631	0.0024221	
0.1741101	0.1313671	0.0993773	0.0753711	0.0573085	0.0333779	0.0151030	0.0069749	0.00421272	0.0015752	
0.1549573	0.1147411	0.0852000	0.0634383	0.0473624	0.0266086	0.0114200	0.0050092	0.0029255	0.0010244	
0.1227407	0.0875354	0.0626245	0.0449413	0.0323491	0.0169102	0.0065294	0.0025837	0.00141083		
0.0972221	0.0667803	0.0460309	0.0318375	0.0220949	0.0107467	0.0037332	0.0013326			
0.0609984	0.0388667	0.0248690	0.0159782	0.0103074	0.0043404	0.0012204				
0.0542883	0.0339477	0.0213212	0.0134485	0.0085185	0.0034601					
0.0303143	0.0172573	0.0098758	0.0056808	0.0032842	0.0011140					
0.0150652	0.0076624	0.0039218	0.0020197	0.0010464						
0.0074869	0.0034022	0.0015574								
0.0037208	0.0015106									
0.0018491										

Appendix C: FVIFA - Period Interest Rates

n	0.3333%	0.4167%	0.50%	0.75%	1.00%	1.25%	1.50%	2.00%	3.00%	4.00%	5.00%
1	1	1	1	1	1	1	1	1	1	1	1
2	2.0033333	2.00416666	2.005	2.0075	2.01	2.0125	2.015	2.02	2.03	2.04	2.05
3	3.01001101	3.01251736	3.015025	3.0225562	3.0301	3.0376562	3.045225	3.0604	3.0909	3.1216	3.1525
4	4.02004428	4.02506951	4.0301001	4.0452254	4.060401	4.0756269	4.0909033	4.121608	4.183627	4.246464	4.310125
5	5.03344429	5.04184064	5.0502506	5.0755646	5.1010050	5.1265722	5.1522669	5.2040401	5.3091358	5.4163225	5.5256312
6	6.05022227	6.06284831	6.0755018	6.1136313	6.1520150	6.1906544	6.2295509	6.3081209	6.4684098	6.6329754	6.8019128
7	7.07038948	7.08811018	7.1058793	7.1594835	7.2135352	7.2680376	7.3229941	7.4342833	7.6624621	7.8982944	8.1420084
8	8.09395720	8.11764397	8.1414087	8.2131797	8.2856705	8.3588880	8.4328391	8.5829690	8.8923360	9.2142262	9.5491088
9	9.12093679	9.15146749	9.1821158	9.2747785	9.3685272	9.4633741	9.5593316	9.7546284	10.159106	10.582795	11.026564
10	10.1513396	10.1895986	10.228026	10.344339	10.462212	10.581666	10.702721	10.949721	11.463879	12.006107	12.577892
11	11.1851770	11.2320552	11.279166	11.421921	11.566834	11.713937	11.863262	12.168715	12.807795	13.486351	14.206787
12	12.2224606	12.2788555	12.335562	12.507586	12.682503	12.860361	13.041211	13.412089	14.192029	15.025805	15.917126
13	13.2632017	13.3300174	13.397240	13.601393	13.809328	14.021115	14.236829	14.680331	15.617790	16.626837	17.712982
14	14.3074119	14.3855591	14.464226	14.703403	14.947421	15.196379	15.450382	15.973938	17.086324	18.291911	19.598631
15	15.3551028	15.4454989	15.536547	15.813679	16.096895	16.386334	16.682137	17.293416	18.598913	20.023587	21.578563
16	16.4062860	16.5098552	16.614230	16.932281	17.257864	17.591163	17.932369	18.639285	20.156881	21.824531	23.657491
18	18.5191757	18.6518906	18.785787	19.194718	19.614747	20.046191	20.489375	21.412312	23.414435	25.645412	28.132384
20	20.6461747	20.8118136	20.979115	21.491218	22.019003	22.562978	23.123667	24.297369	26.870374	29.778078	33.065954
24	24.9428780	25.1859206	25.431955	26.188470	26.973464	27.788084	28.633520	30.421862	34.426470	39.082604	44.501998
28	29.2971572	29.6333863	29.974522	31.028233	32.129096	33.279384	34.481478	37.051210	42.930922	49.967582	58.402582
30	31.4961285	31.8850124	32.280016	33.502901	34.784891	36.129068	37.538681	40.568079	47.575415	56.084937	66.438847
32	33.7097838	34.1554410	34.608623	36.014829	37.494067	39.050440	40.688288	44.227029	52.502758	62.701468	75.298829
36	38.1815397	38.7533357	39.336104	41.152716	43.076878	45.115505	47.275969	51.994367	63.275944	77.598313	95.836322
40	42.7132171	43.4283422	44.158847	46.446481	48.886373	51.489557	54.267893	60.401983	75.401259	95.025515	120.79977
48	51.9595593	53.0148856	54.097832	57.520711	61.222607	65.228388	69.565219	79.353519	104.40839	139.26320	188.02539
50	54.3098635	55.4617634	56.645162	60.394257	64.463182	68.881789	73.682828	84.579401	112.79686	152.66708	209.34799
60	66.2989110	68.0060835	69.770030	75.424136	81.669669	88.574507	96.214651	114.05153	163.05343	237.99068	353.58371
72	81.2224640	83.7642596	86.408855	95.007027	104.70993	115.67362	128.07719	158.05701	246.66724	396.05656	650.90268
84	96.7540194	100.328654	104.07392	116.42692	130.67227	147.12904	166.17263	213.86660	365.88053	649.12511	1184.8448
96	112.918348	117.740514	122.82854	139.85616	159.92729	183.64105	211.72023	284.64665	535.85018	1054.2960	2143.7282
108	129.741229	136.043198	142.73989	165.48322	192.89257	226.02255	266.17777	374.41287	778.18626	1702.9877	3865.7449
120	147.249494	155.282282	163.87934	193.51427	230.03868	275.21705	331.28819	488.25815	1123.6995	2741.5640	6958.2397
240	366.772977	411.033687	462.04089	667.88686	989.25536	1497.2394	2308.8543	5744.4367	40128.420	306130.05	2434771.4
360	694.044455	832.258696	1004.5150	1830.7434	3494.9641	6923.2796	14113.585	62328.056	1394020.8		

6.00%	7.00%	8.00%	9.00%	10.00%	12.00%	15.00%	18.00%	20.00%	24.00%	30.00%
1	1	1	1	1	1	1	1	1	1	1
2.06	2.07	2.08	2.09	2.1	2.12	2.15	2.18	2.2	2.24	2.3
3.1836	3.2149	3.2464	3.2781	3.31	3.3744	3.4725	3.5724	3.64	3.7776	3.99
4.374616	4.439943	4.506112	4.573129	4.641	4.779328	4.993375	5.215432	5.368	5.684224	6.187
5.6370929	5.7507390	5.8666009	5.9847106	6.1051	6.3528473	6.7423812	7.1542097	7.4416	8.0484377	9.0431
6.9753185	7.1532907	7.3359290	7.5233345	7.71561	8.1151890	8.7537384	9.4419675	9.92992	10.980062	12.75603
8.3938376	8.6540210	8.9228033	9.2004346	9.487171	10.089011	11.066799	12.141521	12.915904	14.615277	17.582839
9.8974679	10.259802	10.636627	11.028473	11.435888	12.299693	13.726819	15.326995	16.4990848	19.122944	23.857690
11.491315	11.977988	12.487557	13.021036	13.579476	14.775656	16.785841	19.085854	20.7989017	24.712451	32.014997
13.180794	13.816447	14.486562	15.192929	15.937424	17.548735	20.303718	23.521308	25.9586821	31.643439	42.619497
14.971642	15.783599	16.645487	17.560293	18.531167	20.654583	24.349275	28.755144	32.1504185	40.237865	56.405346
16.869941	17.888451	18.977126	20.140719	21.384283	24.133133	29.001667	34.931070	39.5805022	50.894952	74.326950
18.882137	20.140642	21.495296	22.953384	24.522712	28.029109	34.351917	42.218662	48.4966026	64.109741	97.625035
21.015065	22.550487	24.214920	26.019189	27.974983	32.392602	40.504705	50.818022	59.1959232	80.496079	127.91254
23.275969	25.129022	27.152113	29.360916	31.772481	37.279714	47.580410	60.965266	72.0351078	100.81513	167.28631
25.672528	27.888053	30.324283	33.003398	35.949729	42.753280	55.717472	72.939013	87.4421294	126.01077	218.47220
30.905652	33.999032	37.450243	41.301337	45.599173	55.749714	75.836357	103.74028	128.116666	195.99416	371.51802
36.785591	40.995492	45.761964	51.160119	57.274999	72.052442	102.44358	146.62797	186.687999	303.60062	630.16545
50.815577	58.176670	66.764759	76.789813	88.497326	118.15524	184.16784	289.49447	392.484236	723.46099	1806.0025
68.528111	80.697690	95.338829	112.96821	134.20993	190.69888	327.10408	566.48089	819.223311	1716.1006	5164.3109
79.058186	94.460786	113.28321	136.30753	164.49402	241.33268	434.74514	790.94799	1181.88156	2640.9163	8729.9854
90.889778	110.21815	134.21353	164.03698	201.13776	304.84771	577.10045	1103.4959	1704.10945	4062.9130	14755.975
119.12086	148.91345	187.10214	236.12472	299.12680	484.46311	1014.3456	2144.6489	3539.00937	9611.2791	42150.728
154.76196	199.63511	259.05651	337.88244	442.59255	767.09142	1779.0903	4163.2130	7343.85784	22728.802	120392.88
256.56452	353.27009	490.13216	684.28041	960.17233	1911.5898	5456.0047	15664.258	31593.7435	127061.91	982105.58
290.33590	406.52892	573.77015	815.08355	1163.9085	2400.0182	7217.7162	21813.093	45497.1907	195372.64	1659760.7
533.12818	813.52038	1253.2132	1944.7921	3034.8163	7471.6411	29219.991	114189.66	281732.571	1679147.2	
1089.6285	1850.0922	3174.7813	5490.1890	9545.9381	29133.467	156363.26	832202.70	2511995.49		
2209.4167	4184.6505	8013.6167	15462.202	29980.627	113527.42	836611.57	6064789.2			
4462.6505	9442.5232	20198.627	43510.132	94113.436	442324.24	4476110.1				
8996.5995	21284.259	50882.557	122399.55	295389.66	1723308.7					
18119.795	47954.119	128149.91	344289.06	927080.68	6713993.7					

Appendix D: PVIFA - Period Interest Rates

n	0.3333%	0.4167%	0.50%	0.75%	1.00%	1.25%	1.50%	2.00%	3.00%	4.00%	5.00%
1	0.99667774	0.99585062	0.9950248	0.9925558	0.9900990	0.9876543	0.9852216	0.9803921	0.9708737	0.9615384	0.9523809
2	1.99004426	1.98756908	1.9850993	1.9777229	1.9703950	1.9631153	1.9558834	1.9415609	1.9134696	1.8860946	1.8594104
3	2.98011055	2.97517253	2.9702481	2.9555562	2.9409852	2.9265337	2.9122004	2.8838832	2.8286113	2.7750910	2.7232480
4	3.9668876	3.95867804	3.9504956	3.9261104	3.9019655	3.8780579	3.8543846	3.8077286	3.7170984	3.6298952	3.5459505
5	4.95038631	4.93810261	4.9258663	4.8894396	4.8534312	4.8178350	4.7826449	4.7134595	4.5797071	4.4518223	4.3294766
6	5.93061758	5.91346318	5.8963844	5.8455976	5.7954764	5.7460099	5.6971871	5.6014308	5.4171914	5.2421368	5.0756920
7	6.90759227	6.88477661	6.8620740	6.7946378	6.7281945	6.6627258	6.5982139	6.4719910	6.2302829	6.0020546	5.7863733
8	7.88132120	7.85205969	7.8229592	7.7366132	7.6516777	7.5681242	7.4859250	7.3254814	7.0196921	6.7327448	6.4632127
9	8.85181515	8.81532915	8.7790639	8.6715764	8.5660175	8.4623449	8.3605173	8.1622367	7.7861089	7.4353316	7.1078216
10	9.81908487	9.77460165	9.7304118	9.5995795	9.4713045	9.3455259	9.2221845	8.9825850	8.5302028	8.1108957	7.7217349
11	10.7831410	10.7298937	10.677026	10.520674	10.367628	10.217803	10.071117	9.7868480	9.2526241	8.7604767	8.3064142
12	11.7439944	11.681222	11.618932	11.434912	11.255077	11.079311	10.907505	10.575341	9.9540039	9.3850737	8.8632516
13	12.7016555	12.6286028	12.556151	12.342345	12.133740	11.930184	11.731532	11.348373	10.634955	9.9856478	9.3935729
14	13.6561351	13.5720526	13.488707	13.243022	13.003703	12.770552	12.543381	12.106248	11.296073	10.563122	9.8986409
15	14.6074436	14.5115876	14.416624	14.136994	13.865052	13.600545	13.343233	12.849263	11.937935	11.118387	10.379658
16	15.5555916	15.4472242	15.339925	15.024312	14.717873	14.420292	14.131264	13.577709	12.561102	11.652295	10.837769
18	17.4424482	17.3068665	17.172768	16.779181	16.398268	16.029548	15.672560	14.992031	13.753513	12.659296	11.689586
20	19.3167883	19.1511081	18.987419	18.508019	18.045552	17.599316	17.168638	16.351433	14.877474	13.590326	12.462210
24	23.0282508	22.7938983	22.562866	21.889146	21.243387	20.624234	20.030405	18.913925	16.935542	15.246963	13.798641
28	26.6906368	26.3766026	26.067689	25.170712	24.316443	23.502517	22.726716	21.281272	18.764108	16.663063	14.898127
30	28.5036292	28.1457329	27.794053	26.775080	25.807708	24.888906	24.015838	22.396455	19.600441	17.292033	15.372451
32	30.3045952	29.9002120	29.503283	28.355650	27.269589	26.241274	25.267138	23.468334	20.388765	17.873551	15.802676
36	33.8707664	33.3657012	32.871016	31.446805	30.107505	28.847267	27.660684	25.488842	21.832252	18.908281	16.546851
40	37.3897822	36.7740290	36.172227	34.446938	32.834686	31.326933	29.915845	27.355479	23.114771	19.792773	17.159086
48	44.2888338	43.4229559	42.580317	40.184781	37.973959	35.931480	34.042553	30.673119	25.266706	21.195130	18.077157
50	45.985089	45.0509161	44.142786	41.566447	39.196117	37.012875	34.999688	31.423605	25.729764	21.482184	18.255925
60	54.2990689	52.9907062	51.725560	48.173373	44.955038	42.034591	39.380268	34.760886	27.675563	22.623489	18.929289
72	63.9174367	62.0927774	60.339513	55.476848	51.150391	47.292474	43.844666	37.984063	29.365087	23.515638	19.403788
84	73.1592778	70.7518347	68.453042	62.153964	56.648452	51.822185	47.578633	40.525515	30.550085	24.072872	19.668007
96	82.0393317	78.9894405	76.095218	68.258438	61.527702	55.724570	50.701675	42.529433	31.381219	24.420918	19.815133
108	90.5717613	86.8261075	83.293424	73.839381	65.857789	59.086508	53.313748	44.109509	31.964159	24.638307	19.897059
120	98.7701748	94.2813501	90.073453	78.941692	69.700522	61.982847	55.498454	45.355388	32.373022	24.774088	19.942678
240	165.021858	151.525312	139.58077	111.14495	90.819416	75.942277	64.795732	49.568551	33.305667	24.997958	19.999835
360	209.461240	186.281616	166.79161	124.28186	97.218331	79.086142	66.353241	49.959921	33.332536	24.999981	19.999999

5.00%	6.00%	7.00%	8.00%	9.00%	10.00%	12.00%	15.00%	18.00%	20.00%	24.00%	30.00%
0.9523809	0.9433962	0.9345794	0.9259259	0.9174311	0.9090909	0.8928571	0.8695652	0.8474576	0.83333333	0.8064516	0.7692307
1.8594104	1.8333926	1.8080181	1.7832647	1.7591111	1.7355371	1.6900510	1.6257088	1.5656420	1.52777777	1.4568158	1.3609467
2.7232480	2.6730119	2.6243160	2.5770969	2.5312946	2.4868519	2.4018312	2.2832251	2.1742729	2.10648148	1.9813030	1.8161128
3.5459505	3.4651056	3.3872112	3.3121268	3.2397198	3.1698654	3.0373493	2.8549783	2.6900618	2.58873456	2.4042766	2.1662406
4.3294766	4.2123637	4.1001974	3.9927100	3.8896512	3.7907867	3.6047762	3.3521550	3.1271710	2.99061214	2.7453844	2.4355697
5.0756920	4.9173243	4.7665396	4.6228796	4.4859185	4.3552606	4.1114073	3.7844826	3.4976025	3.32551011	3.0204713	2.6427459
5.7863733	5.5823814	5.3892894	5.2063700	5.0329528	4.8684188	4.5637565	4.1604197	3.8115275	3.60459176	3.2423155	2.8021122
6.4632127	6.2097938	5.9712985	5.7466389	5.5348191	5.3349261	4.9676397	4.4873215	4.0775657	3.83715980	3.4212222	2.9247017
7.1078216	6.8016922	6.5152322	6.2468879	5.9952468	5.7590238	5.3282497	4.7715839	4.3030218	4.03096650	3.5655018	3.0190013
7.7217349	7.3600870	7.0235815	6.7100813	6.4176577	6.1445671	5.6502230	5.0187686	4.4940862	4.19247208	3.6818562	3.0915394
8.3064142	7.8868745	7.4986743	7.1389642	6.8051905	6.4950610	5.9376991	5.2337118	4.6560053	4.32706007	3.7756905	3.1473380
8.8632516	8.3838439	7.9426862	7.5360780	7.1607252	6.8136918	6.1943742	5.4206189	4.7932248	4.43921672	3.8513633	3.1902600
9.3935729	8.8526829	8.3576507	7.9037759	7.4869039	7.1033562	6.4235484	5.5831469	4.9095125	4.53268060	3.9123898	3.2232769
9.8986409	9.2949839	8.7454679	8.2442369	7.7861503	7.3666874	6.6281682	5.7244756	5.0080615	4.61056717	3.9616046	3.2486745
10.379658	9.7122489	9.1079140	8.5594786	8.0606884	7.6060795	6.8108644	5.8473700	5.0915775	4.67547264	4.0012940	3.2682112
10.837769	10.105895	9.4466486	8.8513691	8.3125581	7.8237086	6.9739861	5.9542348	5.1623538	4.72956053	4.0333016	3.2832394
11.689586	10.827603	10.059086	9.3718871	8.7556251	8.2014121	7.2496700	6.1279658	5.2731642	4.81219481	4.0799308	3.3036919
12.462210	11.469921	10.594014	9.8181474	9.1285456	8.5135637	7.4694436	6.2593314	5.3527464	4.86957973	4.1102568	3.3157940
13.798641	12.550357	11.469334	10.528758	9.7066117	8.9847440	7.7843158	6.4337714	5.4509488	4.93710442	4.1428067	3.3271923
14.898127	13.406164	12.137111	11.051078	10.116128	9.3065665	7.9844227	6.5335080	5.5016006	4.96966841	4.1565745	3.3311832
15.372451	13.764831	12.409041	11.257783	10.273654	9.4269144	8.0551839	6.5659796	5.5168059	4.97893639	4.1601031	3.3320610
15.802676	14.084043	12.646555	11.434999	10.406240	9.5263755	8.1115943	6.5905328	5.5277261	4.98537249	4.1623979	3.3325805
16.546851	14.620987	13.035207	11.717192	10.611762	9.6765081	8.1924142	6.6231368	5.5412014	4.99294584	4.1648611	3.3330697
17.159086	15.046296	13.331708	11.924613	10.757360	9.7790507	8.2437766	6.6417783	5.5481518	4.99659811	4.1659029	3.3332410
18.077157	15.650026	13.730474	12.189136	10.933575	9.8969255	8.2971629	6.6585306	5.5535858	4.99920882	4.1665300	3.3333220
18.255925	15.761860	13.800746	12.233484	10.961682	9.9148144	8.3044984	6.6605146	5.5541409	4.99945057	4.1665778	3.3333266
18.929289	16.161427	14.039181	12.376551	11.047991	9.9671572	8.3240492	6.6651459	5.5552852	4.99991126	4.1666563	
19.403788	16.415578	14.176250	12.450977	11.088669	9.9895353	8.3309503	6.6663824	5.5555184	4.99999004		
19.668007	16.541883	14.237111	12.480532	11.103132	9.9966656	8.3327216	6.6666135	5.5555504	4.99999888		
19.815133	16.604653	14.264133	12.492269	11.108274	9.9989375	8.3331763	6.6666567	5.5555548			
19.897059	16.635847	14.276132	12.496929	11.110102	9.9996614	8.3332930	6.6666648	5.5555554			
19.942678	16.651350	14.281459	12.498780	11.110752	9.9998921	8.3333229	6.6666663				
19.999835	16.666652	14.285713	12.499999	11.111111	9.9999999	8.3333333					
19.999999	16.666666	14.285714	12.5	11.111111	10						

Index